SPEAK FOR YOURSELF

John Campbell

BBC BOOKS

Published by BBC Books
a division of BBC Enterprises Limited,
Woodlands, 80 Wood Lane, London W12 0TT

First Published 1990

Reprinted 1990, 1991, 1993

ISBN 0 563 21511 9

Set With Xerox Ventura Publisher
by Pye Campbell Communication Projects, Tillington

Printed and bound in England
by Clays Ltd, St Ives plc
Cover printed
by Clays Ltd, St Ives plc

Contents

Some opening words

Before we begin, I want to make a single point which may not make much sense now, but will keep recurring throughout the following pages. If this book has a theme, this is it: when you are speaking, you can either structure your talk around the subject matter, or around the needs of your audience. If you want to be successful, make the needs of the audience your major criterion. *Always!*

One of the first things you have to learn is to distinguish between what the audience *want* to know and what they *need* to know! They will seldom be the same. You might think that, as the speaker, you know the topic, so you will decide what is going to be said. That probably seems perfectly reasonable, until you look at it more closely.

Take this book as an example, I could put forward a very strong case for starting at the beginning (wherever that may be). Perhaps we should start by discussing the theory of communication, or perhaps, how to research your topic, or we could jump straight in and start by analysing speaking techniques. I could justify any of these starting points by saying, 'This is what you need.' But is it what you want?

If you are anything like the average person who wants to find out about speaking, then the first thing you will want to know about is nerves. So I have a choice. I can either insist that you jolly well take what I think you need, or I can bow to common sense and begin the book by talking about nerves. Guess what the first chapter is about!

1 Managing nerves

Nerves manifest themselves in many ways. Different people get a different range of symptoms. In my own case, my breathing tends to get irregular, my hands and knees shake slightly and I am prone to forget what I was going to say next. Some people get a dry mouth as well. (I get that even when the nerves have gone, so I don't know whether it is the after-effect of nerves or merely the fact that the pubs have been open for some time.) These symptoms – as well as other less obvious ones – are brought about by an increase in adrenalin, which you *need* if you are to perform well. And this raises the question, why try to stop them, even if you could?

Most of us also acquire certain mannerisms when we are under stress: jingling coins, scratching our noses, sniffing, or clicking a ballpoint pen. And we take on verbal mannerisms as well: 'Know what I mean? At this point in time. You know? Like...' We are all susceptible to nervous tics such as these. The insidious thing about them is that we often don't realise we have them. But other people do.

Occasionally we do notice and that triggers a second order of nervous symptoms. Imagine that you have been speaking to a large group of people for a few moments and suddenly, in one of those flashes of transcendental awareness, you realise that you are jingling and scratching and sniffing and clicking. And you feel your knees trembling ever so slightly. And you *know* –

with absolute certainty – that everyone in the room has noticed (and pretty soon they will call their friends in to have a look).

Suddenly you start to sweat. Your hands and knees start trembling more noticeably. Everyone in the room notices that too! You sweat and tremble even more and then... What then? You will have to break into the cycle somewhere, otherwise you will end up as a quivering puddle under the lectern. So, *where* do you break in and *how*?

In fact, you have to break the cycle before it starts. As the gardening folk say, 'Kill the weeds afore they comes up.' The first thing to realise is that we can't stop being nervous. If we have any sensitivity at all then we are bound to be apprehensive about things which are important to us. After all, who knows where the first kiss will lead? Will it result in a polite thank you and good night, or to years of married bliss?

So, we should not be surprised or embarrassed at feeling nervous. Indeed, a few nerves will often heighten our perception and our judgement. That is why one should never rely on dutch courage to help us overcome our nerves. Drink and drugs might seem to calm our nerves, but only because they deaden our awareness; they make us *think* we are working well. (Drink drive accidents and countless broken marriages are testimony to the fallacy of that impression.) Then again, if you are speaking formally for the first time, you already feel vulnerable, so why make matters worse by diminishing your capabilities. Why risk being found drunk in charge of an audience?

You *will* and *should* feel nervous at big occasions if you care about what you are doing (ask any experienced actor, politician, after-dinner speaker, or salesman), but that does not mean that you should show it. So the real question is, how do you *manage* your nerves?

Managing nerves

Checklist

Step 1: Examine your fears

☐ What precisely is the fear?

☐ How likely is it to happen and what will you do if it does?

Step 2: Prepare yourself

☐ Know your role and your reasons for talking

Step 3: Starting to speak

☐ Regulate your breathing

☐ Relax your face and neck muscles

☐ Establish eye contact

☐ Occupy your hands

☐ Start your opening ritual

STEP 1: EXAMINE YOUR FEARS

The problem has two components: firstly, what is causing the nervousness? And, secondly, how do we deal with the symptoms? Let us look at the causes first, then we can go on to deal with the symptoms.

Try to examine *why* you are nervous. It is very easy to generalise here and say something nebulous like, 'Nerves are nothing more than fear of the unknown.' But statements like this, however well-intentioned, are of little help.

What precisely is the fear?

Only you can answer the question, 'What is it that is worrying me?' And you need to give yourself honest answers. To help you do this, here are the dozen most common answers which I have heard over the years:

1   I couldn't talk about anything for more than two minutes!

2   I'm worried I might dry up.

3   There may be someone there who knows more than I do.

4   I might leave out an important point.

5   There may be an awkward customer in the audience.

6   I might get asked a question I can't answer.

7   My accent makes me sound stupid.

8   I don't want to let the audience down.

9   I don't think I can string the words together sensibly.

10   I don't want to look daft.

11   I'm just not cut out for it, I don't have the gift of the gab.

12   I've done it before and I was dreadful!

I don't know how many of these responses match your honest answers, but I would be surprised if none of them did. In any case, the best way to deal with any problem is to confront it, so let's examine these twelve most common fears one by one.

Identifying the root causes of our nervousness is merely the first step. We have to examine these causes to see how valid they are. Is there any basis for our fears? How likely are they to occur? What will we do if the worst happens? We have to think through the situations before we can hope to deal with them. So let's hold our fears up to the light to see if they have any substance.

How likely is it to happen and what will you do if it does?

(If you have fears which do not appear in the list, then you might like to go through the same procedure for them by yourself.)

■ *1   I couldn't talk about anything for more than two minutes!*

If I asked you to tell me your favourite joke, or asked about your holiday, or what you thought about the present government, then I am sure you could and probably would talk for more than two minutes. So perhaps we ought to reword the response as, 'I couldn't talk for more than two minutes about *this* topic to *that* audience!' This is easier to deal with, though we still need to improve our definition of the problem.

What is it about the topic that bothers us? Assuming that we know it well, is it that we don't know where to start? Or how to string the ideas together? Or what to leave out? Or where to put the emphasis? Take heart, because these are the very things that will be dealt with in this book.

As for the audience, what is it about them which bothers us? I suspect that the answer is contained in one or more of the remaining eleven responses, so read on.

■ *2   I'm worried I might dry up*

Yes, this could happen. In fact, I will go as far as saying it *will* happen to you one day, so the real question is not 'what will I do *if* I dry up?' but rather 'what will I do *when* I dry up?' The first thing to realise is that drying up is not peculiar to you. It happens to the most experienced 'performer'. But the difference is that experienced speakers do not try to hide the fact by waffling, apologising, or blustering. They know that drying up is a perfectly natural event; they are not surprised or embarrassed when it happens and know that once they get going again all will be well. So experienced presenters usually fall back on a predetermined routine which manages the temporary crisis and gives them a 'kick start'.

The actor will look at the prompter, the teacher will ask if there are any questions, the comedian will trot out his catchphrase and the politician will carry on talking about something else.

So when it happens, what should you do? If you have forgotten which point comes next, then simply look at your notes. Your audience expects you to look at your notes from time to time. What is more, they will probably be reassured to see that you are taking care to check things as you go along. If you have forgotten the actual words you were going to use, don't panic! As long as you remember the idea or the concept you were about to cover, then you can express the same idea in different words; ideas are more important than a particularly neat turn of phrase. If the thing which has gone walkabout is a particular quotation or a set of figures then, here too, look at your notes.

Above all, take your time. Remember, your adrenalin will be pumping and one of the effects of adrenalin is that it seems to expand time - seconds can seem like minutes. The silence that falls when you stop speaking will exert a huge pressure on you if you are not used to it, especially when it seems to go on for ever.

You will get hot around the ears and you will feel as if the eyes of the audience are burning into you, but it will be a false impression. Put yourself in their place. When you are in an audience, you are quite happy to wait for the presenter. In fact you expect to be led; to work at the presenter's pace. So why should your audience feel any differently about you? The moral is, don't let the silence fluster you.

■ *3   There may be someone there who knows more than I do*

I am always a little puzzled when this one comes up, but it is a very common response. Taking it at face value, I suppose the first question which occurs to me when I hear it is, 'If they know so much about the topic, why are they in the audience? Why aren't they giving the presentation?' But what people most often mean by this response is that there may be someone in the audience who knows a lot more about a particular specialist section of the presentation. This does happen quite often. But in such circumstances you, as the presenter, should treat the specialist as a resource, not a threat. Specialists can add to your message, so enlist their help at the appropriate time.

The message here is, 'Know your audience and know what you are trying to achieve.' You must lead the audience, so don't let the specialists take over. When you get to the point where their specialist knowledge becomes relevant, ask them a direct question, listen carefully to the answer, summarise their answer, thank them for their help and then carry on with the next point. Never forget that you start with the advantage of being the presenter and, as such, everyone in the audience – including the specialists – will *expect* you to set the pace. Indeed, if you don't take the lead, you will unsettle and unnerve the audience. But if you try to bluster and show the specialists that you know more than they do, you will simply create antagonism.

■ *4   I might leave out an important point*

The key question here is, what do you mean by an 'important' point? Is it something you rather fancied saying, or is it something which is essential to your audience's understanding of the topic? Do you suspect that you are particularly forgetful? If so, you can guard against most eventualities by designing your notes to suit your own peculiar needs. (See Chapter 4.)

■ *5   There may be an awkward customer in the audience*

This is true. There *could* be someone who challenges your position (which you already see as being shaky); someone who is noisy, cocky, or disruptive. But there are techniques for dealing with them (as you will see). Such people often act the way they do for reasons which have nothing to do with your talk, so don't confuse their problems and inadequacies with your own feelings of insecurity. The chances of you meeting someone who has deliberately set out to destroy your talk are very very slight.

In twenty or so years I have encountered only one person who fell into this category and who had the strength of purpose to try to carry it through. His reasons for trying to spoil the session had nothing to do with me, nor anything directly to do with the course I was running at the time. He left the course during the lunchbreak on the first day.

Let us be realistic though: you will meet people who are intent on being the life and soul of the gathering; people who have an axe to grind; and people who feel they have to prove themselves. That's life! As I said just now, we shall be examining techniques for handling them and getting them to work with you. For the time being, just remember that, as the speaker, you start with the advantage.

■ *6   I might get asked a question I can't answer*

Well, if the question concerns the main subject of your talk, then it serves you right for not researching your topic properly! But if the question is about an obscure point of detail, then what is wrong with saying something like, 'I don't know. That point has never occurred to me before. Why do you ask?' Then you must decide if continuing with the point will contribute to your talk or detract from it.

It seems to me that the mark of the true specialist is that he or she is not frightened of saying 'I don't know.' We often feel that we should have all the answers to every conceivable question, but is that reasonable? I think not. By the way, we shall also be discussing how to handle questions later (see page 103).

The golden rule is: if you can't answer a particular question don't try to bluff it out. *You* can tell when someone is floundering and so can your audience. Admit that you don't know (you can't be expected to know everything) and if the point is worth pursuing, promise to look for the answer after the session has finished. Make sure you keep your promise!

■ *7   My accent makes me sound stupid*

Okay, so you live in 'an ouse' instead of 'a hise', or nowadays perhaps 'a hise' rather than 'an ouse'. Why should that make your knowledge and experience any the less valuable?

My own view, having listened to some fairly profound and wise things said in broad regional accents, is that accent adds colour and interest to the words. Dialect, on the other hand, can be confusing, because it involves words which might be unfamiliar to the audience. The same goes for jargon. So, provided the ideas are worth listening to and the words are familiar to the audience, the accent rarely detracts from a presentation. Indeed the characteristic music and lilt of an accent often enhances it. Never try to hide your accent, or you could end up sounding ridiculous, and hideous:

'Mai waif tells me she positively dislaikes 'am an hegg.' 'Is this a deggar wot I see befaw me?' 'The parish council 'ave desaided to call an 'alt to it, forthwith.'

Don't try to be someone else – leave that to actors; they do it for a living and it takes *them* a long time to do it convincingly. Be yourself and let your ideas speak for themselves.

■ *8   I don't want to let the audience down*

I have always seen this response as a good sign. If you are concerned about the well-being of the audience, then you are less likely to let them down. Many of the problems arise when speakers do not care enough about the audience. And in any case, if you get to know the audience and if you are clear about your objectives, why should you let them down? Perhaps the concern arises because of your lack of knowledge about speaking techniques? If so, read the rest of this book!

■ *9   I don't think I can string the words together sensibly*

Even if you are right, which is unlikely or you wouldn't have been asked to speak in the first place, this book should help. We shall be covering techniques for assembling and organising your material as well as how to create memory joggers.

■ *10   I don't want to look daft*

To help you overcome your natural shyness, think about what your audience needs rather than what might or might not happen to you. Their needs are paramount. And do not forget that the mere fact that you are the speaker means that you start your presentation with a good measure of credibility. You may *feel* daft, but if you do your job properly you won't *look* daft.

■ *11   I'm just not cut out for it, I don't have the gift of the gab*

The last thing a good presenter needs is the gift of the gab. Your presentation should not consist of aimless chatter; it should set out to achieve a clear purpose. For that you will need a reasoned, disciplined and objective approach. Some people adopt such an approach quite naturally, but the rest of us have to learn the techniques – and make no mistake, the techniques can be learned. Hence this book.

■ *12   I've done it before and I was dreadful!*

How do you know you were dreadful? You probably *felt* dreadful, but then you know where you made the mistakes; where you meant to say things and forgot; the fact that you ran out of time; the examples you didn't quote. The audience would not have known those things.

As far as they were concerned you covered every point you meant to cover, in the right sequence, within the time limits. And the effect on your audience is the only real measure of your performance.

Ideally, you should enjoy the session and you should achieve your objectives. If you don't enjoy the session, but still achieve your objectives, that is sad and we need to change it, but the end result is still acceptable. If you thoroughly enjoy the presentation, but don't achieve your objectives, that is a distinct failure; you are guilty of going on an ego trip rather than communicating your message.

So where does all this analysis get us? You should be able to see a pattern beginning to emerge. We can combat our fears by being very clear about two things: firstly, the way we go about the business of speaking (the actual procedures we adopt) and, secondly, the way we view our role as a speaker.

STEP 2: PREPARE YOURSELF

You would not go on a journey without a fairly good idea of where you were going, how you were travelling and when you ought to arrive. You would know the major landmarks along the way and you would be able to tell if your travel plans were going wrong. Going on a journey is a good analogy for the process of presenting information. The matter is first mooted, for instance, as, 'I want you to go to Tenby' – you will probably have only a vague idea where Tenby is. ('It's over there on the left somewhere.') So you begin by consulting the map and identifying the best route. Then it occurs to you to ask, 'Where in Tenby and why am I going?' Once you know these things, then you can start to make your detailed plans. By car or train? When do I set off? Shall I take sandwiches? These are the practical details which help you turn the plan into reality.

The procedures in this book involve the same kind of down-to-earth decisions. They are designed to put you in control of the situation so that you always know where you are, where you are going and, therefore, what you need to do next.

■ *Know your role and your reasons for talking*

We all have to play different roles at different times in our lives. We are like transformer toys – the loving parent leaves the family home and becomes the aggressive commuter fighting for a place on the tube. Striding into the office, the commuter changes yet again into the captain of industry; Jim Kirk urging his crew on to boldly split infinitives. Then, when the boss calls a meeting, the brave captain becomes the cautious adviser. And this goes on for the rest of the day – indeed the rest of our lives!

We expect people to play particular roles in particular circumstances. And other people expect us to play the right role at the right time. If we do not fulfil their expectations we unsettle them. So when you step up to start your talk the audience will have certain expectations of you but, more importantly, they will also have an idea of the role which *they* are expected to play.

What are these roles? In very general terms, the audience is seen as being subordinate to the speaker while the speaker is talking about his or her topic. If you put yourself in the position of a member of the audience, I think you will agree with the following points:

- A speaker is expected to set the direction and pacing of the talk.
- They are assumed to be competent until they do something which casts doubt on that assumption.
- They are assumed to know where they are going, and have good reasons for doing things in a particular way, until they do something which casts doubt on that assumption.
- They are assumed to be competent. Note that word, 'competent', *not* 'perfect' or 'infallible'.
- They are assumed to be confident.

When you step up to start your presentation this is the role you are expected to fulfil. Notice that you are given the benefit of the doubt on all the important things, so you don't have to prove yourself!

What does the audience expect its role to be? The audience expects to be led – sometimes to quite a surprising extent (but we can discuss that later). It expects to work at the pace of the speaker. Most importantly, its members expect to be given guidance as to what precisely the speaker expects of them!

In short, if you approach the task of speaking in a disciplined way, and you are aware of what is expected of you as well as what you can expect from the audience, there is no reason to feel exposed and insecure when you start to speak. Certainly, you will and should feel the effects of your adrenalin – at least for the first few minutes – but you can use that extra energy for your own ends, if you go about it in the right way.

Adrenalin has a whole range of effects on the human body. Among other things, it affects our breathing, blood pressure, senses and perception (of things like time, for example). When people talk about close calls they have had, they nearly always say something like, 'It all happened in a couple of seconds, but it seemed like hours – everything seemed to be happening in slow motion.'

So, what can you do to control, if not harness, the effects of adrenalin? Let us examine one of the most trying situations – speaking to a group of twenty or so people you have never met before.

STEP 3: STARTING TO SPEAK

Regulate your breathing

There are many reasons for doing this but, most importantly, you need to breathe comfortably if you are going to speak at all naturally. A gulp in the middle of a sentence is a sure sign that you feel under pressure and it will unsettle you too. To control your breathing, follow these simple steps:

- Just before you step up to speak, take a few moments to stand or sit quietly.

- Breathe in through your nose, counting slowly to four, then stop. Hold the breath for a further count of four and then release it gently through the mouth.

- For the next breath, try to extend the count to six, or eight. Hold the breath for four seconds again and then release it gently.

- Now try counting to ten or twelve while you breathe in, and then perhaps to sixteen.

- Do not try too hard. Concentrate on establishing a steady comfortable rate of breathing which gives you the air you need, but does not cause you to over-oxygenate and get dizzy.

- If you are prone to sniffing, blow your nose before you step up.

▆▆▆▆▆ Relax your face and neck muscles

These muscles may be a little tense, though the mere fact that you are regulating your breathing will tend to relax them. To relax more positively, follow these simple steps:

- Tense the muscles in your shoulders and neck and then relax them; do it two or three times slowly. Imagine your shoulders coming up around your ears and then slowly falling into a relaxed and normal position.

- Tense your face muscles into a grimace and then relax them. Some people find it helps if they chew an imaginary toffee. You will feel totally foolish while you do these things, but they do help you to feel and look relaxed!

▆▆▆▆▆ Establish eye contact

Force yourself to look directly at the members of the audience – not above their heads, not at where you think they ought to be, not just to one side. Look at people's eyes! Establish contact. It will help you realise that you are talking to people and not to some half-imagined group of monsters. And the human contact will make you feel more at home in itself. It also looks good because the audience will read your action as that of a person who is ready to begin, but has the good manners to check that his audience are ready too.

Many people find this eye contact hard going. My advice is always the same. Just try it once and you will see what I mean. It will make you feel better and it will help to settle you down.

▆▆▆▆▆ Occupy your hands

If your hands have a tendency to shake (as mine do) don't hold your notes. Put them down on a nearby surface where you can see them if you need them. 'Ah,' I can hear you saying, 'what do I do with my hands then?' A lot of people like to hold on to something to stop their hands flying off in all directions as if they have a mind of their own. One solution may be to grasp the sides of the lectern, but then your nerves are betrayed by two neat rows of brilliant white knuckles.

Don't put your hands in your pockets – well not yet anyway! It looks as if you don't care if you do it at this stage. My solution (and it may work for you) is to have one of those fat magic marker pens which I hold behind my back (that way no one can see the white knuckles). I can grip it as tightly as I like to help me channel and focus my nervous energy. The net result is a picture of someone who looks calm and relaxed.

Start your opening ritual

You need a predetermined and well-rehearsed opening ritual to get you through the first two or three minutes of your presentation. This is something we shall be discussing in detail (see page 86), so I shall go no further for the moment other than to say that it will provide you with a familiar haven in an otherwise foreign environment. You will be able to relax more quickly and get into your natural stride.

Be aware that the nervous tension due to the adrenalin will pass quite quickly. As you work through your opening ritual your heart will stop pounding, your breathing will settle itself down and you will stop trembling. It takes no more than two or three minutes. Then you are sailing! You can forget about your problems and get on with the job in hand.

2 Preparing your talk

Having dealt with the subject of nerves, you are now ready to prepare the talk itself. But how do you decide what you are going to say? And how do you know where to begin? How are you going to handle your audience? And at what level are you going to pitch your materials? The questions seem to be endless.

In this chapter we shall be examining how to prepare yourself so as to prevent problems coming up and throwing you off your stride. Of course some problems will still arise no matter how carefully you plan, but at least they can be minimised.

As with so many activities, the talk itself is merely that 10 per cent of the iceberg which sticks up above the water. What keeps it there is the 90 per cent you can't see. A flawless presentation depends far more on careful planning and preparation than it does on virtuoso speaking skills. Certainly we should be concerned that our speaking technique is up to scratch (see Chapter 7), but we must not ignore the fact that a successful talk calls for expertise in a whole range of other skills as well.

So picture yourself being asked to give a talk to the local Women's Institute, or making a presentation at a sales conference, or attending an interview for a job. Where do you start? What do you do first?

Preparing your talk

Checklist

Research

☐ Define the purpose

☐ Know your audience

☐ Define objectives

☐ Know the setting and conditions

Analyse

☐ Analyse the subject matter in the light of all the above

RESEARCH

The checklist for this chapter itemises a set procedure which you should work through whenever you have to give a talk. It applies just as much to making an important phone call as it does to talking to a hall full of people. Try to cultivate the procedure until it becomes almost a reflex action. After a while, as soon as you know you have to give a presentation or a talk, you will automatically run through the key questions one after another. In plain English, ask yourself, 'Why am I talking? Who am I talking to? What do I need to achieve? Where am I talking? What should I say?'

For a quick 'off the cuff' talk you can more or less answer these questions in a matter of seconds. But for a more detailed and longer presentation you might take several days to work out all the answers. All communication processes involve a series of decisions and the whole point of approaching the task in a systematic way is to let the method force you to make decisions in the right order.

In my experience of using this 'reflex procedure' for designing courses, writing books, technical manuals, audio scripts and the like, these activities account for about 30 per cent of the time I spend on any one job. So if I spend three weeks designing and writing a fairly complicated talk, then one week of that time will have been spent on basic research along the lines we shall examine now. Without this discipline, I am not sure that I could get the job done so quickly or so effectively. As before, let us examine the items on the checklist one by one.

Define the purpose

When people ask you to talk, they are generally very vague about what they want. The interviewer will say, 'Tell us about yourself.' It is up to you to decide what to tell him or her. Being somewhat mischievous I am quite often tempted to say something like, 'I'm six foot tall, I have a forty-four inch chest, I weigh fifteen stone, I play rugby, I like mountain climbing, bull wrestling and wearing little black frocks', just to see what happens. Similarly when the boss says, 'I want you to talk to some customers about your job', there are endless possibilities. You could talk about the working conditions, or how precisely you stick those little plastic thingies into that other plastic thingy, or the people you work with, or the management, or the machinery you have to use, what you think about the career prospects and so on.

So when you are first approached to talk about a topic (or indeed if you volunteer yourself) two questions should pop into your head unbidden: 'Why am I talking about the topic?' And 'Who am I talking to?' (the first two headings on this checklist). It is not enough to have a broad topic heading for the talk, such as 'Yourself' or 'Your work'. The person who is asking you to talk may have one theme in mind while you have a completely different one.

As we have seen, both you and your audience need a clear purpose for the talk. I was once called in to write a technical handbook because the company who had been given the original contract had spent three months writing the wrong manual for the customer. They had done a marvellous job of writing a detailed reference manual when the customer actually wanted a training manual. The customer refused to pay for the work, the company threatened to sue and it all got very messy and expensive. Luckily this happened fairly early in my career and I was able to learn from someone else's misfortune. As a result I vowed that the same thing would never happen to me and I devised the procedure we are looking at now.

If someone says, 'Tell me about yourself', you should, therefore, respond by saying, 'Certainly. Where would you like me to start?'. If someone says, 'Talk to some customers about your job', then you should ask, 'Fine, which particular aspects would they like to know about?' If you decide to make a phone call to complain about your new video recorder, ask yourself, 'What am I actually complaining about? Is it that the recorder seems to be a tapivore (it eats tapes), or is it that the man who installed the recorder has sold me some dodgy tapes?'

In one sense it is understandable that people do not want to be very specific when they ask someone to give a talk. They expect the speaker to know the subject matter and they don't feel they should dictate to a specialist. But how can the specialist be expected to know why the audience wants to know about the subject matter? Someone has to be more specific about the task. Most often it will be you. So, what sorts of things must you consider?

Know your audience

Put simply, the most important single element of any communication process is the audience. They should determine everything you do; they should guide every decision you make. Most professional communicators will tell you the same thing if you ask them to identify the most important factor in their work: the journalist will say that the readers are all-important; the teacher will say that the pupils or the students are paramount; the salesman will cite the customers; the entertainer will cite the audience, and so on. At first glance there would seem to be almost universal agreement on this point.

But if you look a little more closely you find some puzzling contradictions. I have worked with a wide range of professional communicators. And when we discuss this point - 'the audience is the most important single element of a communication process' - everyone in the room does an impression of one of those little nodding dogs which used to live in the back windows of Morris Minors. Everyone agrees wholeheartedly and no doubt sincerely. Yet, if I asked those same people to tackle a practical problem, and then watch what they do, their behaviour often does not match their professional convictions.

You might like to try the same exercise. Imagine that you are sitting down, minding your own business and someone approaches you and says, 'Will you please give a talk to our accounts department to show them how the new computer system works'.

How would you set about the task? Jot down on a piece of paper a list of the things you would do in the order in which you would do them. This is not a trick question, so be honest. If your first reaction is to panic, well put that down as the first item on your list.

The vast majority of people know very little about computer systems (which is why I chose it as the topic for this exercise), so we find that the first significant activity on most people's lists is researching the topic; they begin by finding out as much as they can about how the computer system works.

But why? If we really believe that the audience is all-important and the audience determines everything we do, shouldn't we start by finding out as much as we can about them?

If we begin by researching the topic, we are forced to research the *whole* topic, even the bits we will not need for the talk. This means that we will waste a lot of time and effort. Even worse, allowing the topic (rather than the audience) to dominate our activities will reduce the efficiency of the communication in other ways concerning the 'logic' of the talk we are developing.

For example, when we decide where to start our talk how do we do it? 'Easy,' you might say, 'you start at the beginning.' True enough, there must be a natural, or 'logical' starting point for any topic, but that logical starting point is different for different people. For the topic of computers one speaker may take binary numbers as the starting point, another may choose the work of Babbage, yet another may choose the main functions and components of a computer, and so on. These are all valid starting points if you shape your talk around the nature of the topic – if your talk is 'topic centred'.

But how many computer users give a hoot about the history of computing engines, or how computers count? They do not need the information; any more than the present-day rail commuter needs to know about the development of trackways in Elizabethan Britain. The great danger with centring your talk on the needs of the topic is that you waste your own time and that of the audience with irrelevant detail. And if the audience cannot see the relevance of what you are saying, then you are likely to lose them.

If, on the other hand, your first action is to look at what your audience already knows about the topic, what it needs to know, what it wants to know and how it will *use* the information, then you are far less likely to waste time during the preparation and delivery phases of your talk. So the first step should be to research the *audience;* leave the topic until later.

Many people react to this suggestion by saying, 'Ah yes, but I don't know who I'll be talking to' or 'Every audience is different' or some other equally valid-sounding objection. But it is amazing what you can find out if you simply refuse to give the talk until you get some information from the person organising it. Of course, there will be times when there is a very little information available. On such occasions I feel rather exposed and vulnerable so I always begin my presentation by trying to find out some key facts about the audience.

Actually it is very seldom the case that you know absolutely nothing about the audience – an audience of housewives is quite different from an audience of football hooligans. The trick lies in defining the difference as closely as you can. This means gathering together the information you do have and, more importantly, identifying the key facts you *don't* have. Here is a list of the questions you might ask about the audience.

■ *About the audience*

- How many people will there be?
- What one word or phrase would describe them?
- Do they have any previous experience of the topic?
- Are they used to getting information via the spoken word?
- Will they respond better to a practical approach or to a theoretical approach?
- Will they be looking for facts and figures or for general principles?
- Are they attending out of choice or under orders?
- Will they want to listen?
- What is their likely attitude toward the topic?
- What is their age range?
- Will there be a 'status' range?
- Will they have specialist knowledge of any aspects of the topic?
- What will they want to do with the information I present?

Try to get inside the head of your audience - under their skin. It makes for a lumpy audience, but try to see things from their point of view. Remember, you should never think of the audience as 'dummies': they will be of at least average intelligence; they just happen not to know much about the topic. Never patronise an audience; unless, of course, you fancy being lynched, either metaphorically or literally!

So at this stage we know the purpose of our talk (e.g. to show the accounts department how the computer system works) and we should have at least a thumbnail sketch of the audience (along with a list of key points we still need to find out). In other words, we know *why* we are going to talk and we know *who* we will be talking to. But we still don't know what we want the outcome of all this work to be.

We never communicate simply to communicate. We communicate in order to change things in some way: to increase people's knowledge, to provide them with new skills, or to change their attitudes or emotions. So the next thing we need is a precise statement of *how* we want the audience to be changed by what we say.

Define the end result

People often say, 'This step is a waste of time, I've already said what I'm going to do, when I defined the purpose!' And yes that is true, they have said what they are going to do. But that, by itself, is not enough. We must also be concerned about what *the audience* is going to do as a result of the talk.

It seems to me that there is no point in doing any job unless you do it well. But how do you tell a good job from a mediocre job, or even a bad job? We need measures of some kind, but what exactly is it that we should be measuring? Should we be measuring the process - the talk itself - or should we be measuring the product - the end results of the talk? Remember, we don't give a talk, just to give a talk; there is usually a sound reason for presenting information to people.

You could say that we give a talk because we want to change the audience in some way: perhaps we want to increase their knowledge about a topic, or get them to accept a proposition, or maybe we just want them to be entertained.

It makes sense then, that we should measure our success by measuring how the audience has changed, rather than by measuring our speaking technique; i.e. measure the product, not the process!

But before we can measure how the audience has changed, we need a very clear definition of how we *want* the audience to be changed. And the more detailed that definition the better. Let's go back to our computer example for a moment, so I can illustrate what I mean.

If we had simply stated our purpose as: 'to show the accounts department how the computer system works' and gone no further, how would we tell if our talk has been successful? When we use the 'purpose' as our yardstick the only thing we can measure is the quality of the presentation - how well we showed the accounts department. That, by itself, does not tell us if the accounts department actually understood what we said. We might well have given a very impressive looking talk, but still be guilty of missing the point - like producing an award winning advert which fails to sell the product.

The only real measure of our success has to be what the audience will do as a result of our talk. For example, that they will be able to *operate the new computer system*; or perhaps, that they will *volunteer for specialist training* in the new system; or even that they will *raise no objections to the installation* of the new system. In fact there could be any number of reasons for giving a talk which has the purpose we stated. That is precisely the problem!

Knowing precisely *what* you are going to do (the purpose) and *why* you are going to do it (the objective or objectives), gives you the speaker's equivalent of a compass bearing and a map. If you keep the purpose and the objectives clearly in your sights you will not be tempted to stray off course. Once we know the purpose of the talk, how do we define our objectives?

For every-day practical purposes we can usually confine ourselves to simply defining what we want the audience to be *able to do* (though purists would have it differently). We must define it in terms which are easily measurable. This usually means that it must be *concrete* rather than abstract. But it must also be *reasonable* to expect the audience to do it and it must be practically *possible* for them to be able to do it; concrete, reasonable *and* possible – all three elements are essential!

For example, turning water into wine may be measurable, but is it *reasonable* and *possible* for ordinary mortals? Expecting your audience to understand your report on what went wrong with the computer system might be reasonable and possible, but 'understand' is too abstract a term to be measured easily. Of course you can do it, but only by defining other, more concrete, indirect measures. To 'understand' is a fudge term, here are some others to steer clear of: 'be aware', 'know', 'appreciate', 'approve of', 'learn', 'agree with' ... and countless others.

Always think in terms of what your audience will do as a result of your talk, in fact, when you sit down to list the objectives (there is usually more than one), write these words at the top of a blank sheet of paper: 'At the end of my talk the audience will...' Then, one by one, list the things which they will be able to do.

Once you know precisely where you are going and what you have to achieve along the way, then you can start to design your material for the talk, confident that you will include everything you need to achieve the objectives. Equally importantly you will be able to exclude everything which does *not* contribute directly to achieving the end result you want. It should follow that everything you say in your talk will have a point and you will be able to eliminate aimless wanderings.

In my experience, when speakers have a clear idea of what they are trying to achieve, they project an image of someone who's on the ball; of being organised and in control, knowing what they want and how to get it. If you can develop the knack of approaching the talk objectively, your audience – and you – will have increased confidence in your abilities.

Know the setting and conditions

The setting and the conditions can and should affect your talk in a number of ways. First, you need to consider the obvious (and not so obvious) physical conditions.

How big is the room? I once had to give a talk in a very large room when I had all but lost my voice. Fortunately, I had already established that the room was large and it had a PA system, so I was able to take a throat microphone with me.

What distractions are there? There are nearly always distractions in any venue. Some are worse than others: traffic noise, people walking up and down a corridor outside the room, an air conditioning system that makes rude noises, wonderful paintings on the wall, a clock ticking slowly and loudly, a clock immediately behind the speaker, even sunny weather. All of these can work against you.

I once attended a seminar given by a very high-powered and somewhat opinionated speaker, who was waxing pompous about his theories on how people learn. He was a little man dressed in muted earthy colours, sporting a huge black beard and enough hair for several friends. I couldn't see his feet because they were hidden by the lectern, but I feel certain that he must have been wearing sandals - and beige socks. Behind him was a complete wall of glass which looked out on to lawns and fountains. Some way into his presentation – with the audience already shifting in their seats with irritation – just as he was reaching a crescendo of dogmatism, a very serious looking window cleaner walked purposefully across the lawn into centre stage behind the speaker, propped his ladder against the window and began to wave his chamois leather at the audience while whistling silently. Pretty soon people were screaming with laughter. I forget what the speaker was trying to tell us, but I did enjoy his session.

There were several sources of distraction in that sorry tale. I should tell you that the speaker was addressing a group of thirty or so industrial training managers, almost all of whom were over the age of fifty and had retired from one or another of the services after successful careers in training.

The first thing which unsettled the audience was the speaker's physical appearance. I am not saying that his appearance was wrong, but I am saying that it did not conform with the audience's expectations. The next thing was the speaker's attitude and style of presentation. He made no allowances for the audience's knowledge and solid practical experience, he simply ignored it and proceeded to give the lecture he would normally have given to his second-year students at a polytechnic.

The third source of distraction was the glass wall behind the speaker's dais and the lawns and fountains beyond. The fact that it was a sunny day was, in itself, unusual enough to be a further distraction. Then there was the interaction within the group: shared glances of amusement turning to disbelief and then hostility. The speaker failed to spot any of them. In the event, the whistling window cleaner probably saved the speaker's 'self esteem' (as he would have called it). He was the safety valve which averted an almost certain explosion; and only just in time.

There is often very little you can do to eliminate distractions, but you have to find some way of compensating for them. For example, imagine that you are in full flow, just about to make a key point and a fire engine goes by outside. What do you do? Many inexperienced speakers try to compete by raising their voices in an attempt to drown out the noise of the siren. Meanwhile the audience will be listening to the siren, trying to tell if it belongs to a police car, a fire engine or an ambulance; the fact that the speaker is shouting fit to bust is just an irritation.

The experienced speaker, on the other hand, will have been monitoring all aspects of the environment and will have been the first one to hear the siren approaching. When the siren is close enough to distract the audience the speaker will stop and wait for it to pass. As it dies away, they will grab the audience's attention again, perhaps by sharing the old joke, 'He won't sell a lot of ice cream going at that speed!' Then the speaker will quickly summarise, to remind people of the point they had reached, then continue with the talk.

The inadequate speaker I mentioned just now could have eliminated nearly all of the distractions working against his talk. He could have pulled the curtains to block out the glass wall. He should have found out about his audience and modified his style of delivery. And he could have combed his hair and perhaps put on a tie: not because it was right, but because it was what the audience expected and because every other speaker had taken the trouble to do so. In short, the speaker created all the problems for himself, because he did not take steps to find out about the setting and the conditions for his talk.

So how do you compensate for the most common distractions when giving a talk? Here are some ideas.

■ *Traffic noise on a hot day*

Open the widows before your presentation, but close them just before you begin to speak. The sudden reduction in noise will sound like silence and will signal to the audience that you are about to start. Make sure that you open the windows to circulate the air during breaks in your presentation.

■ *People walking up and down outside the room*

There is very little that you can do about this, other than be aware that it will distract your audience. If someone walks by just as you are making a critical point, make sure that you repeat the point (using different words) after they have gone.

■ *An air conditioning system that makes rude noises*

In many ways air conditioning systems create some of the greatest problems - there is so little you can do to compensate for their surreal effects. It is distracting for the speaker too; how do you react when you see someone's wig lifting ever so slightly each time the system switches itself on?

I have two ways of dealing with dodgy air conditioning. The first is to share the joke with my audience - it is funny for a while and we can all laugh together, but before long it ceases to create hilarity, fades into the background and stops being a distraction. The second way of dealing with problematical air conditioning is to switch it off in the room. This is not such a good method on a hot day, because before long you will have to open the windows and then you have traffic noise problems instead.

■ *Nice pictures on the wall*

Obscure them if you can by placing chart stands or a screen in front of them. If you can't obscure them, make a point of bringing them to your audience's attention, remark on how nice they are and then, either literally or metaphorically, say, 'Well that's enough about them, let's get on with the job'.

■ *A clock ticking slowly and loudly*

This one is particularly problematic immediately after lunch. The slow tock ... tock ... tock heightens people's desire for sleep. You need to compensate for this by 'turning up the volume' on your own presentation. Increase the pace and the tempo. Present the information in smaller lumps. Use more summaries. Move about more. Use diagrams to illustrate your points. Do everything you can to shake the audience's shoulder.

■ *A clock immediately behind the speaker's head*

This one can be so demoralising! It is very bad for the ego to stand in the centre of the 'stage', basking in the rapt attention of the audience, only to find that when you move to one side, their eyes stay firmly fixed on the front of the room where the clock is.

As with the pictures, try to obscure the clock by placing a projection screen in front of it. If that is not possible, move the speaking position to one side of the stage. If that can't be done either, sneak into the room before the audience arrives and tape a piece of card over the clock face.

■ *Sunny weather*

In Britain the merest glimmer of sunshine can cause quite a stir ('It's summer outside, why am I stuck here listening to this twit?'). But of course there are other side effects. The temperature will usually rise, so you may have to do something about ventilating the room - or compensating for the roars and gurgles coming from the air conditioning. If the audience is facing a window or a bright part of the room, you will have to give them a break from time to time, to stop them getting headaches. Also, you might find that your presentation aids are lost in the glare. If the sun is streaming in on people's backs then you may have to pull a curtain or allow people to move. And you will have to allow for the fact that some of the audience may be getting uncomfortably hot.

All in all, the setting and conditions can affect your talk in many ways. But if you remember that you have two options – eliminate or compensate – then you will be able to live with most situations.

ANALYSE

Analyse the subject matter in the light of all the above

Notice that it is only now that you need to start looking at the topic for your talk. By now you will know *why* you are speaking, *who* the audience is, *what* your talk should achieve and the *conditions* under which you will be giving the talk. So now you can begin to answer these two questions:

- Which parts of the subject matter do the audience need if they are to do what I want them to do?

- Allowing for the setting and conditions, how should I present that information?

Let's look at a few examples of real situations and how you could tackle them, using this method.

■ *Before a phone call*

The purpose of my call is to book a holiday, so what information will I need to give to the holiday firm? As it is lunchtime, they are likely to be busy and understaffed, so I'll make it quick.

■ *Before a meeting with the bank manager*

I want this loan so, how do I persuade the manager that I am credit-worthy? The meeting will be on his territory, his chair will be higher than mine and I'll be facing the window, but I won't be intimidated. I shall present the facts calmly and with confidence.

■ *Before making an after-dinner speech at the cricket club*

I want to make the members laugh, but at the same time I want to pull them together as a club so, what jokes can I make and at whom should I aim them? They may have had a few drinks, the toilets are through that squeaky door at the back, and those people that are still awake will want to get on with the dancing, so I had better start with a bang, get the presentations over and done with and finish by firing my best joke at the captain of the first team.

■ *Before showing the accounts department how the new computer system works*

I want the accounts staff to see how the new system will make their jobs easier, so I do not need to give much detail about how to operate the system. I need to stress how it will impinge on their work and highlight the ways in which it will reduce their workload without threatening their security. The meeting will be held in one of the conference rooms, so we will be on neutral ground, but I must make my talk down-to-earth and practical so they can apply the information to their own jobs.

Here you can see how the same procedure works for a range of situations - the more complex the problem, the longer the analysis, but the actions and questions involved always remain the same. The answers to these two key questions will provide you with a thumbnail sketch for your message, a sort of rough draft. It is the equivalent of the drawing on the back of an envelope, which is where every good idea starts life.

Armed with your sketch you can now go on to develop the finished product.

3 Structuring your talk

Deciding what not to say is usually the most difficult part of preparing a talk. If you know the subject very well, then it is hard to know what to leave out. In many ways it is easier to design a talk on a topic you know nothing about - at least you can see the wood for the trees. However, if you approach the job in a disciplined way, you can let the system do a lot of the work for you.

If you look at the checklist on the next page, you will see that it has five deceptively simple-looking steps. For many people this is the 'make or break' stage of the whole process of giving a talk. The structure of your presentation is critically important. A badly structured talk presented with consummate skill is often still a bad presentation. Whereas a well- structured message will get its main points across despite the presenter. If the message 'hangs together' both you and your audience you will be able to keep track of things.

This is the procedure I use for preparing talks and presentations, and writing scripts, courses, books and manuals. It is quite normal for me to start a project knowing nothing at all about, for example, the computer or the software system I am writing or talking about. In this sort of situation I have to use a systematic approach to make sure I get things right. It has to be a system I can trust and I'm pretty sure it will work for you too.

Structuring your talk

Checklist

The framework

☐ Identify the main elements and sub-elements of the topic

☐ Choose a starting point

☐ Find the 'best' route through the material

Movable parts

☐ Find analogies to clarify unfamiliar ideas

☐ Use examples and illustrations to support the message

THE FRAMEWORK

◾◾◾◾◾ **Identify the main elements and sub-elements of the topic**

If you are going to talk on any subject you will not be able to transmit all the information at once, in one big lump. You will have to break it into bite-sized chunks. So straightaway you are going to have to be selective. Somehow you will have to decide where to take the first bite (and we shall deal with that in the next section). But even before this you will have to decide what it is you are biting and how big each bite should be. Just how do you do this?

Your audience holds the answer. If you look at the subject matter through *their* eyes, then you should be able to see a pattern and it will be a pattern which will make sense to them. For example, imagine that you are going to give a talk on basic car maintenance to a group of secondary school children. You can assume that most of of the audience will know little or nothing about cars. They will not want to know how they work and they may feel apprehensive about the technology. Let us also add that they will not be familiar with motoring jargon and are likely to be put off if it intrudes at all.

That seems like some problem. But is it? Let's start by looking at the topic itself, through the eyes of the audience.

Every topic has several 'layers' of information – like the skins of an onion. Your task, when you are presenting a topic, is firstly, to uncover the layers which are relevant to the audience and secondly to describe them in terms which the audience will understand. You can choose to analyse the topic either by what it *is,* or by what it *does.* My advice is that you analyse the topic by what it does, because the audience will find that easier to understand. Let me explain why.

When you stand back and look at anything – no matter how complex – you will see that it exists because it does something specific. It performs a (small) number of useful 'functions'. This seems to be equally true for a car, a washing machine, a computer program, a management planning system and many other topics. Indeed, I have not yet found one to which it does *not* apply.

If you begin your analysis by listing the major functions of the topic, you will have uncovered the first layer of information. For example, for a car you might list:

- To transmit power smoothly from a power source to the wheels.
- To carry passengers in comfort and safety.
- To change direction at will.
- To stop quickly and safely.
- To be suitable for use both during the day and at night.

Somewhere between three and six major functions is fairly typical and most audiences can cope with this number of ideas at once. If you have come up with less than three, see if you can break one or two of them down into more detail. If you have come up with more than six, see if you can group some of them together.

Remember, we are concentrating here on what a car *does,* not what it *is.* This is an important distinction. In other words, try to get back to the very first sketch on the back of an envelope that someone drew when they had the original idea in the back room of a pub.

The motor car did not come into being with someone saying, 'Today I think I'll invent an internal combustion engine and I'll put a clutch on the back of it and then a gearbox, fix a prop shaft onto that and then bolt the whole shebang to a differential gear...' It is much more likely that someone said, 'Phew, my feet hurt! Wouldn't it be nice if there was something that could carry me and my carrots to market. If I had a set of wheels, and something to push or pull them, and seats, and some way of avoiding potholes, and some way of stopping it running away down hills, and some way of seeing in the dark so I could get to market early and come back late, then that would be a good thing.'

If the inventor had a reason for creating the thing in the first place and made sense of it by describing what exactly it should do, it seems logical that we should follow suit when we come to examine the thing later. We need to start our analysis by asking, 'What is it for?' and, 'What does it do?'

If you try to understand a car, or any other 'system', by producing a list of the major components, it makes the the whole thing that much more complicated. To go back to our car example again, a car is a device which has the following components:

- Engine.
- Ignition system.
- Fuel system.
- Cooling system.
- Lubrication system.
- Transmission.
- Braking system.
- Electrical system.
- Steering system.
- Safety equipment.
- Seating and interior trim.

Now we have eleven items – a much less manageable number – *and* you have to understand some of the jargon to make sense of the list itself. Of course, the novice will not know the jargon ... All in all, it seems far more helpful to examine what the system *does* rather than what it *is*, particularly if you look at it through the eyes of your audience. Let's look at some other examples.

■ *An automatic washing machine through my eyes*
What does a washing machine do?

- It holds clothes, water and washing powder or liquid.
- It ensures that the clothes are thoroughly immersed and agitated in the soapy water for a set time.
- It gets rid of the dirty water and takes in clean water to rinse the clothes.
- And finally it gets rid of most of the water left in the clothes after the rinse.

In broad terms that describes an automatic washing machine using ideas that even I can understand.

■ *My computer through the eyes of a complete novice*
What does this computer do?

- It enables me to get information into its circuits.
- It processes that information for me.
- It enables me to get the processed information out again.
- It enables me to keep permanent copies of my work.

■ *My computer through the eyes of a 13-year-old computer expert*
If we examine the same computer through the eyes of a different audience, we will come up with what looks like a different result.

- It enables me to input information using a keyboard, a mouse, a scanner and a floppy drive.
- It will run any software designed for DOS 2 upward.
- It outputs data to an EGA screen, a laser printer, a hard disk drive, a floppy disk drive and a modem.
- It stores data on a 40 megabyte hard disk and a 1.2 megabyte floppy disk and I can fit a tape streamer.

The second description uses different language and it has a bit more technical detail, but it is essentially the same as the first one, which demonstrates why it is important to do the analysis through the eyes of a specific audience. From the outset you will treat the information in terms which will make sense to *them*.

The broad descriptions we have looked at so far are simply the first step in the process. If we imagine the topic to be a tree, so far we have the trunk – the name of the topic – and we have four or five main boughs. We now need to identify the branches and possibly the twigs. In our example of the car seen through the eyes of schoolchildren these were the 'boughs':

- To transmit power smoothly from a power source to the wheels.
- To carry passengers in comfort and safety.
- To change direction at will.
- To stop quickly and safely.
- To be suitable for use both during the day and at night.

Taking just one of these functions, we can extend the analysis. Let's take the first one on the list, 'To transmit power smoothly from a power source to the wheels'. Under this heading we can group the following tasks or branches:

- To provide power.
- To control the power supplied by the source.
- To connect the power source to the wheels.
- To alter the gearing to compensate for changes in the terrain.
- To interrupt the transmission of power to the wheels, e.g. to change gear or to stop.
- To maintain the power evenly when the car is turning.

We could stop there, but what about tyres? They could be included here, but it might be better to include them under the second or the fourth bough. Where precisely you slot the information is not as important as making sure that you have a sound reason for putting it where it is. In this context a 'sound reason' is one which will make sense to the audience!

We now go through the same process for the other main boughs until we have identified all the branches for each one. Then we break the information down into even smaller units, one branch at a time. The important thing is that, even for the tiniest twig on the topmost branch of the topic, you should be able to trace an unbroken route all the way back to the trunk. That way your information tree has a trunk and boughs which the audience will recognise and each of those will lead on naturally to the next level of information.

How do you know when to stop? Well, if the audience determines the shape of the tree, your purpose and your objectives will determine its size. And this is why clear objectives are so important. The acid test is, 'Will this piece of information help me achieve my objectives?' If you know the topic really well, a better question might be, 'If I omit this information will it stop me from achieving my objectives?'

You are unlikely to come up with a perfect tree at the first attempt. In practice you will often find that you have started off by identifying the wrong boughs, so you scratch out what you have done and start again. The next one will be better, but it will probably still benefit from a bit of tinkering and fine tuning. Eventually you will end up with a tree which looks right, and makes sense to the audience.

This activity may involve three or four stages, but don't assume that it takes a long time. Certainly it takes a long time to describe the process, but that is surely understandable. In reality you can construct an information tree in seconds if you have to.

Imagine yourself sitting in a seaside bar on a Greek island, chatting to someone you have just met. One of the first things they will ask you is, 'What do you do?' You answer by giving your job title. This will prompt the question, 'Oh, what does that involve?' Our conditioning leads us to think in terms of the tasks we perform, so your initial response may be either to tell the person to mind their own business, or to reel off a long and boring description of precisely what you do on a typical day. On the other hand, if you are feeling very relaxed and you decide not to be a complete bore, you will make light of the question and answer with a vague description of the four or five reasons why your job exists (its functions). You can formulate your answer in less than a second. And if you can do it in conversation, it means you can do it in more formal circumstances.

Follow your instincts rather than your conditioning. Why should a more formal situation demand a different approach from the one we use all the time? As always, when you are analysing information, concentrate on the needs of your audience, rather than the constraints of the topic itself.

Choose a starting point

A logical starting point is logical only if the *audience* sees it as such. I know that sounds like something out of a Christmas cracker, but it is still worth remembering.

The simplest, and often the best, way to present the tree is to begin at the trunk, then describe the main boughs, then move on to describe the branches, and so on. If you have done your analysis through their eyes, then the audience should be able to follow what you say. But this is not always the case, and sometimes it is not the *best* strategy.

For example, if your talk is a sales presentation, then you may want to *end* at the trunk rather than begin there (i.e. end with the real sales proposition – the 'punchline'). But in the majority of cases the straightforward answer is to use the shape of the tree itself as the pattern for your message. In which case, your analysis will have given you your starting point. Like this perhaps:

Good morning children. Today we're going to look at motor cars. I think you'll be surprised if I tell you that, even though they seem complicated, cars actually only do a few simple jobs. Now you may say that they only do one job, carry you and me where we want to go, but we need to look more closely than that; they have to carry us in a particular way. For a start, we want to be comfortable and safe ... and your mum or dad has to be able to steer around corners and things ... And stop if someone runs out into the road without looking! You want a nice smooth ride as well; you don't want to be jerked about all over the place. And lastly, we want to be able to use the car at any time, night or day. That's only five jobs in all. Let's look at them one by one ....

Find the 'best' route through the material

So you have decided that your best strategy is to start at the trunk and work upwards and outwards. In our motor car example, as soon as you start climbing the trunk you come to the point where the five boughs lead off in different directions. You can't climb them all at the same time, so which one do you choose to climb first? If there were a *right* one for every topic things would be easy, but life isn't like that.

You have to assess the situation by asking yourself, 'Which one of these alternatives relates most closely to the previous experience of my audience?' The answer to that question will give you a bearing, but there are other things to consider. For example:

- Which of the boughs will the audience want to climb first?

- If I deal with that part of the topic first, will the audience be able to understand all the ideas?

- Will I be able to lay foundations in this section of my talk for items which will come later?

- Should I continue straight out to the branches and twigs of this section, or should I deal with all the other boughs first, followed by all the branches and then the twigs?

- Given the circumstances under which I shall be giving the talk, is one of the boughs more appropriate than the others?

In order to answer these questions you must have a good idea of the nature of your audience, the shape of the information tree, your purpose and objectives and the setting and conditions for your talk. The same goes for all the subsequent decisions you will have to make.

MOVABLE PARTS

Find analogies to clarify unfamiliar ideas

Analogies are very powerful tools, but they have to be used carefully. They enable you to describe the essential elements of an unfamiliar concept in terms which the audience will understand. It is important that the analogy you choose should be appropriate.

For example, I used the analogy of an 'onion' to illustrate that when you *analyse* a topic, you uncover several layers of information. But when I talked about *presenting* the information, I chose another analogy – that of a 'tree' – in an attempt to make the abstract concept seem more concrete. I could have used other analogies, I could have talked about the 'root system of a tree'; it is the same basic shape and structure as the tree, but I did not think it was the best analogy because I wanted to use the idea of people working upward and outward as they gained knowledge of the topic. Also, we all know and understand words like bough and branch and twig, whereas I have no idea what the equivalent parts of a root system are called.

The essential elements of a good analogy are that it should be known to the audience and that it should provide a reasonably similar picture to the thing you are describing. Ideally it should generate the right emotional responses in your audience and it should not generate harmful ones.

■ Use examples and illustrations to support the message

Words are all very well, but they are nothing more than a medium of expression and they can be misinterpreted. They are the paint with which we create a picture of our ideas. But the picture may be very dead. To bring the subject of your talk to life you will need to provide examples and illustrations, to add perspective and depth.

If you are being interviewed for a job and you say you are used to taking responsibility, that is pretty boring. But if you give at least one example it sounds far more impressive. If you were describing how to get to a particular building in the heart of London, you would draw a map. If you were describing your prize-winning turnip, you would use your hands to demonstrate the size and perhaps let your knees buckle a little to signify its weight.

You can illustrate your talk without pictures, but examples have to be real, or at least realistic. Like analogies, they must also be things your audience will understand. Wherever possible give examples of real life objects or events. Before you choose an example or an illustration make sure that you have a real reason for using it. Do not use it simply because you feel you ought to. Examples must have a specific job to do: to reinforce something you have said, to highlight detail which would otherwise be missed, to show an interrelationship, to summarise. These are just a few of the possible reasons for using examples, illustrations and analogies. If you can, try to use appropriate examples from your own experience; they are so much more credible.

4 Memory aids

You are a very lucky person if you can give a talk without any notes to jog your memory. And you are a very crafty person if you can make it *look* as though you are not using any notes. There is nothing wrong with letting your audience see you using notes, but it looks marginally more professional if you seem to be talking 'off the cuff'.

In this chapter we shall look at how to prepare notes and support materials to suit your style. And we shall see that there are ways of 'cheating' by preparing materials which support your message and jog your memory at the same time.

Memory aids

Checklist

☐ Prepare a 'route map' through the topic

☐ Identify key words and phrases

☐ Prepare your notes

☐ Prepare support materials

Prepare a 'route map' through the topic

In the previous chapter we saw how to *select* a route through the subject matter. In fact, you should prepare your route map as part of that process and I have separated it out here only to emphasise it as a different activity. Having planned the best route through the topic, your objective now is to *record the results* of the planning process. You can record the route in a number of ways.

For example you could produce a diagram of the information tree annotated with numbers to remind you of the presentation sequence. Or you could write a series of checklists, much as I have done in this book. You might want to make a list of headings and sub-headings. Or you could draw up a detailed timetable for your talk with specific time slots allocated to particular sections of the topic.

When I am presenting courses lasting one, two, or three days, I usually draw up a grid for each day and set aside the required amount of time for the main sections of the course: half an hour for introductions and opening ritual, two hours for the section on presentation techniques, an hour and a half for feedback, half an hour to summarise the day's work and give 'a trailer' for the next day's, and so on. I try not to be too specific about time, because I know that during the course I will gain time on some sections and lose it on others.

It is far more important to have some sort of map, than to worry about its precise form. Use the style that suits your way of working. The route map is nothing more than a statement of intent. Its job is to remind you of the next point on the list, it is not designed to remind you of what you are going to say about that point. For some people the map may be all they need to jog their memory and keep them on course. This is particularly likely if the speaker knows the topic very well or if he or she has given the same talk time and time again. But its real purpose is simply to point towards the next step on the route.

Identify key words and phrases

If you are giving the talk for the first time, you will probably need something more than a list of headings. You may need something which will remind you of one or more of the items listed on the following page:

- The objective for the current part of the presentation.
- The main point you are covering and the ideas or facts you want to mention at this stage.
- When to use a presentation aid, and which one you should use.
- How much time should have elapsed at this stage of the talk.
- The precise wording of a quotation, or a particular set of statistics which you want to quote.
- Examples and analogies and perhaps the wording of questions which you want to ask the audience.

Don't be tempted to write a script (I shall explain why in the next section). Instead, concentrate on producing a list of key words or phrases which will jog your memory. Try to keep this list of key words to a minimum. And trust your memory.

The important thing about your memory aids is that they should hold enough information to trigger your memory, but not so much information that you can't find the bit you want. It will take a while to get this balance right - it is different for different people.

Perhaps the best answer is to produce two sets of key words for a brand new talk: one set which contains the absolute minimum you think you can get by with, and another set which holds the amount of detail that makes you feel comfortable. Start your talk by using the minimal set and see how you get on. If you find as you get into the talk that you need more help, switch to the comfortable set. I think you might be surprised at how little help you need.

Minimalism has two main advantages. Firstly, there is less visual clutter so you can find your place more easily. And secondly, having to make up the words as you go along forces you to be more immediate and spontaneous, so that your own character shines through the words. For the audience this is infinitely preferable to listening to a speaker who is hiding behind a hedge of prepared statements.

This method can be used for the majority of verbal presentations. However, there may be times when you are asked to give a talk to strict time limits (for example on the local radio station), or you may be asked to present a carefully worded statement which must be delivered precisely, or even to provide the commentary for a video or slide show. On such occasions you probably will need much more than a list of key words or phrases.

At this stage we are merely drawing up a list of key words or phrases in the same sequence as the route map. You will need a key word or phrase for each junction point – each turn and fork in the road.

A route map is actually a very good analogy for this process. Some years ago I worked for Pickfords Heavy Haulage who specialised in moving 'abnormal loads'. (If it wasn't bolted down, they would move it!) Shifting a 150 ton lump from Hayes in Middlesex to a power station in the wilds of Scotland was run-of-the-mill stuff. It was part of my job to find routes for loads such as this and then write up the driver's instructions.

We would begin the driver's instructions with a rough description of the load and a starting and finishing point for the journey. We would know perhaps 60 per cent of the route from previous experience. Hayes was a common starting point and we knew the best practical route from there, to the North Circular Road, to the A1 and on up to Scotch Corner. The difficult bit – the bit that was unknown to us – would generally be at the other end of the journey where we had to find a practicable route from the main trunk roads through to the South Gate of the Invercockyleeky B power station.

The first 60 per cent of the route was a formality. As far as the drivers were concerned it could have been expressed as 'Get to Scotch Corner by the A1 route.' The key phrase – the one which triggered the memory for the drivers – was 'the A1 route'. Once they saw those words, they knew the rest. They knew departure times, they knew the hazards along the route, they knew where and when to park either for crew changes or to meet police escorts. That one phrase summed it up for them, because they had done the run so often.

The Invercockyleeky end was a different proposition; we would have to provide far more detail and we might use diagrams as well as words. But even here, we still adopted a form of shorthand using key phrases: '.... approaching town centre ensure that street furniture has been removed, cross to the right-hand carriageway, TL at crossroads. Police assistance required.'

Those few words probably summed up half an hour's hard and skilled work. It was easy for us. All we had to do was write the routes. The drivers had to cope with traffic problems, police liaison, public relations, local authority liaison, water boards, electricity boards, impatient motorists, British Rail, stray cattle, breakdowns and many other things which could and did go wrong. Our route notes were meant only to guide them and perhaps warn them of particular hazards and how to deal with them. They knew their jobs and, provided they had the right triggers, they would get the load through without mishap in virtually every case.

And so it should be with your presentation notes. Concentrate on key words and phrases which make sense to you, perhaps like this:

```
                    The Car
    Five main functions
    1. Carry load  2. Power source  3. Steer
    4. Stop  5. Use day and night


    1. Carry load
              comfort
              safety
              luggage


    2. Power source
              petrol      (reciprocating, rotary)
              diesel
              control     (throttle, choke, etc.)


    3.      (etc.)
```

Prepare your notes

Once you have your list of key words or phrases you may decide to use the list itself in place of your notes – I quite often do – but you also have a range of other options open.

■ *Conventional notes*

Write your notes on an A4 sheet of paper. You should be able to get the notes for quite a long session (say, thirty minutes plus) on a single sheet of A4. Of course, it depends a bit on how big your writing is. You can use colour coding to separate out the different major sections. When you come to give your talk, put the paper on a table or lectern. It's not a good idea to hold the paper. If your adrenalin makes you tremble slightly, the length of the paper will magnify the tremble and make it seem like a shake. As we have seen, this may unnerve you and the audience.

■ *Index Cards*

Transcribe the notes on to index cards with one card for each major section of your talk. Index cards are easy to handle and fairly robust. They are also quite small, so, if your hands have a tendency to shake, it is less noticeable with cards. Don't put each card down on a separate pile when you have finished with it. Take it from the front of the pack and move it to the back, so you always have the same number of cards in the pile. That way your audience won't be tempted to waste their time and attention trying to work out how many cards are left in the pile (and therefore how much longer you will be).

There are many ways of 'cheating' (disguising the fact that you are using notes). Here are just a few.

■ *Overhead projector transparencies*

If you use an overhead projector (OHP), pencil your notes on the frames which hold the transparencies. Better still, if you can, use the transparencies themselves as your notes.

■ *Flip charts*

Pencil your notes on the corners of a flip chart. If you do it lightly, you will be able to see what you have written, but the audience will not. As far as they can tell, when you turn the page, the sheet is blank, ready for you to write on. For a fairly informal talk, you can lean nonchalantly by the flip chart without the audience ever knowing the real reason for your casual stance.

■ *Hidden notes*

Use a rather large name card and put it at the front of the desk or the lectern. The audience will be able to see your name, but not the notes on the back of the card.

In all of these examples you are using one of your normal 'stage props' to do at least two jobs – its usual job and the unexpected one of providing you with a memory jogger. And remember, the fewer notes you need, the easier it is to hide them.

When we first start to speak in formal circumstances, we all tend to over-prepare. We either prepare too much for the available time, or we make the notes so precise and complicated that we become scared of losing our place. Somehow the notes become more important than the job they are supposed to do.

I remember a case on one of my courses where a recent graduate had to give a talk, the purpose of which was to persuade a selection panel (the rest of the group) to employ him. When he was running through his school and university history he stumbled and stuttered, checking his notes before every sentence. After a few minutes of this, I persuaded him to turn his notes face down. He carried on with the talk, but this time he was fluent, he sounded more certain of his facts (which, of course, he was) and, because he had to construct a storyline to guide his own thoughts, he suddenly provided the audience with a storyline as well. In short, his performance improved dramatically.

I suppose the extreme case of over-preparing is to write a detailed script for a presentation. There are times when a script is necessary, but they are relatively few and far between. Some examples would be, a speech at a conference, reading a paper at a seminar, or a political speech which has been circulated to the press beforehand, but how many of us will ever experience situations like those? My advice would be to avoid scripts like the plague. Remember that we are talking about communicating via the *spoken* word. Spoken English (or French, or German, or Chinese) is quite different from the written version. Let me demonstrate. In the previous chapter I wrote these words:

> If you are going to talk on any subject you will not be able to
> transmit all the information at once, in one big lump. You will
> have to break it into bite-sized chunks. So straightaway you are
> going to have to be selective. Somehow you will have to decide
> where to take the first bite, (and we shall deal with that in the
> next section). But even before this you will have to decide what
> it is you are biting and how big each bite should be. Just how do
> you do this?
>
> Your audience holds the answer. If you look at the subject
> matter through *their* eyes, then you should be able to see a
> pattern and it will be a pattern which will make sense to them.

Appropriately enough, this is in written English, albeit in a chatty
style. If you were to try reading it aloud it would sound a bit
stilted and forced. Here is the same piece written in spoken
English:

> If you're going to talk on any subject, you won't be able to say
> everything at once, in a big lump. You'll have to break it into
> bite-sized chunks. Straightaway you'll have to be selective.
> Somehow you'll have to decide where to take the first bite (we'll
> look at that in a minute). But before you can do *that,* you'll have
> to sort out just what it is you're biting... and how big your bites
> should be... But how...?
>
> Your audience holds the answer. If you look at the subject
> through their eyes, you should be able to see a pattern... a
> pattern that'll make sense to them.

If you try reading this version aloud you should find the words
easier to say. In fact it is still fairly grammatical. Everyday speech
tends to be much more disjointed, with half-finished sentences
and odd sentence constructions. That is why speaking the written
word sounds so false and distant, and even insincere. Writing
natural-sounding scripts is a lot harder than it looks and it always
seems to take a lot longer than you expect. And reading a script
in front of an audience without sounding false is an equally
difficult exercise.

There is one further problem which comes from working with scripts: if you lose your place, or get the pages out of order, or turn over two pages at once, you are in deep trouble.

So if you are tempted to write a script for your talk, remember that it will take a lot longer than you expect to produce a narrative that sounds natural and relaxed, and you will need to rehearse the speech several times to get it exactly right. Then you will have to stand in front of the audience and use an actor's skills to do the script justice. There is no real room for error. I'm far too lazy to volunteer for that much work, particularly when there is a better and easier way to get superior results.

Prepare support materials

Virtually all 'talks' need support materials of some kind. For a phone call it is wise to have a pad and pencil handy. For a job interview you may need a birth certificate, proof of qualifications, driving licence or references. For an interview at the bank for a loan, you'll need facts and figures of various kinds and if it is a business loan you will need a business plan and cash-flow forecasts. An after-dinner speech might require a list of jokes and maybe some props such as a dunce's cap or a French maid's uniform (I didn't say what kind of dinner it was). For a sales meeting you will need brochures, leaflets, samples and possibly a detailed written proposal. To talk to children about cars you will need diagrams and pictures and possibly models. The list goes on and on.

At this stage you should simply decide which support materials you will need, what job they should do and when precisely you should use them. Later in the book we shall look at some tips and tricks for how you might use them (see Chapter 5).

5 Support materials

Describing a spiral staircase without moving your hands is nearly as difficult as eating a doughnut without licking your lips. Somehow when we talk about fairly complex objects or emotions we have a natural desire to enhance our words – sometimes words are simply inadequate for the job we want them to do. We need props or support materials to help us express our thoughts and our audience needs them so they can interpret our ideas more accurately and easily.

In this chapter we shall examine why we need support materials and how we can use them to best effect. This general overview applies to all kinds of support materials, including visual aids, models, mock-ups and computer simulations, which all share many characteristics.

Support materials

Checklist

Preparing the material

☐ Have a clear purpose for the material

☐ Make sure that the material is clear and legible

☐ Use layout as part of the message

Using the material

☐ Know when to use the material

☐ Make sure that everyone can see the material

PREPARING THE MATERIAL

▐ Have a clear purpose for the material

Never use support materials just because you think it might be nice to have them. Remember you are giving a talk which has quite specific objectives, and the support materials are there to support your message – in other words to add power or impact to what you are saying. Art for its own sake has its place, but not in your talk. So you need to ask yourself why you want to use support materials and what they can do for you. A few of the more obvious uses are listed below.

■ *To reinforce a point you have made*

If people can see as well as hear the information then they are more likely to remember it, particularly if the support material makes the same point in a different way from the spoken word. For example, if you mention that exports increased by 50 per cent during 1986 and 1987, then a very simple illustration (see below) will act as a trigger.

People will remember the sudden step in the bar chart, which gives them a way of remembering the rest of the point.

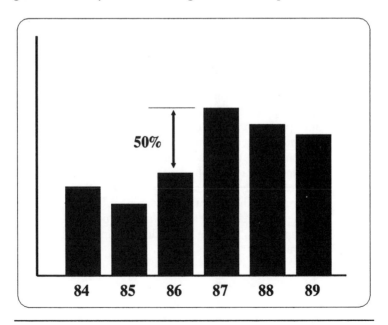

■ *To show what something looks like*

Assuming that you are describing something physical, rather than abstract, the best way is to show the audience the actual thing you are describing. But that might cause problems if your talk is about the dams in the Eland Valley. Second best is a model of some kind, third best is a photograph, followed by a drawing and then a diagram. (It is sometimes dangerous to assume that your audience will be able to read diagrams. Quite a lot of people find them difficult to work with.)

■ *To illustrate relationships*

If you are describing an abstract topic, such as a management structure, or the tactics for a game of football, or something which is hidden from the audience's view, like the water control system within one of the dams in the Eland Valley, then a picture will help your audience envisage the system you are describing. It will make it more tangible for them.

■ *To show information patterns*

This is an extension of the previous point. Sometimes you will want people to see a pattern in the information you are presenting, because the *pattern itself* is important. For example, if you are analysing a writer's style, you could highlight certain word patterns which are typical of his work, or if you are reporting back on a traffic study, then one of your main illustrations must be how traffic patterns vary during the day.

■ *To interpret a set of figures*

Usually when we make a point which is supported by statistics or other figures, the numbers themselves are unimportant; it is the interpretation which matters. Also, many people (me included) are put off by lists of numbers. If the numbers show, say, a trend of some kind, then it's the trend that needs to be illustrated: a sloping line on a graph gets the point over much more quickly and effectively than a set of figures. For example, you may want to bring out the point that sun spot activity goes through a cycle with roughly eleven years between the peaks. Here you could use a graph, a bar chart or some clever graphics to make the point for you.

■ *To record the proceedings*

Some talks, particularly those designed to brief people on a project, or to agree tactics, or to examine a particular problem in a group, will benefit from support materials which record the points *as* they are made. The record will organise the contributions and stop people from going over the same ground time and time again. It will also focus attention and prevent them from straying off the point. So if you are going to talk at such a meeting you may like to display the main headings for the meeting (the agenda) at the start of your talk, filling in the spaces between the headings as you go along.

■ *To summarise the key points*

A good summary can also reinforce, draw out relationships, show patterns, illustrate trends and record proceedings. In addition it can provide 'punctuation' as we discussed earlier. Use summaries as one of your standard tools. Including them in your support materials in some way will sharpen their cutting edge.

■ *To act as your notes*

In Chapter 4 (page 55), we saw how to use this method of 'cheating', so I shall say no more about the topic now.

These then are the most common uses for support materials. Any one item may do several of the jobs, and most of them do more than one. There are many valid reasons for using support materials, but you should always make sure that you know precisely why you are using them. If you do *not* have a sound reason – such as the ones I have listed – do not use the material, because it may 'compete' with your message.

Make sure that the material is clear and legible

Clarity and legibility are of the utmost importance, especially when you give a presentation in a large room. In this section we shall examine the main things you need to bear in mind.

■ *Amount of information*

Do not present too much information at once. This is a very common fault, indeed it is *the* most common fault! For example, imagine that you are talking to the bank manager, or to the committee of a club and you want to put forward an idea based on, say, an analysis of costs and prices. In your efforts to be totally honest you may be tempted to present all the relevant figures.

This is inadvisable for several reasons.

Firstly, the audience is very seldom interested in all the figures. At most they are interested in totals and sometimes they are interested only in the conclusions you have drawn from the totals. Secondly, the figures are boring and, for some people, confusing. I know that when I am confronted by neat columns of numbers, my first reaction is to stick my head under the blanket and wait for them to go away. Thirdly, your support materials should have impact - that is how they support your words.

Too much information is like a snowstorm; there are too many individual flakes to make any sense, in fact, there are so many that they tend to 'white out' the scenery. You should be using a few snowballs to get your points across; they will have much more effect. Ideally you should not try to present more than two or three main points with any one item of support material.

■ *Size*

Make sure that the information you present is big enough to be seen clearly by everyone in the audience. This is another reason for not presenting too much information in one go. The more you present with any one item of support material, the less room there is for each individual item of information and so the smaller it has to be.

■ *Clarity and contrast*

Make sure that text is written in block capitals, that the lines of your drawings are thick enough to show up and that there is lots of 'contrast' in any images you present. Try producing a sample, then go to the back of the room and check that you can see all the information.

■ *Colour*

One way of contrasting points is with colour. Remember that we are conditioned to 'read' colours. Here is how we might interpret a few colours.

- Red   = danger! or hot!
- Green   = safe or natural or good
- Blue   = cool or water
- Purple   = wealth
- Yellow   = warmth or sunlight

So, if you are using a flip chart and you want to transmit an unwritten message that one of the items in a list is good and another is bad, put the name of the good item in green and the bad item in red.

You may be tempted to use the colour red to signify importance, for example, by showing a list in which the major headings are in red and the lesser items are in some other colour. It depends on the marker you are using, but red is not often the strongest colour available to you. Remember, if you want something to stand out as being important, then it should contrast with its surroundings.

On a flip chart, or an OHP transparency most of the surroundings will be white, so black has greater contrast than red. In fact blue is probably the best choice, because it has good contrast, it is a strong colour *and* it has the right psychological effect.

Colour has a greater effect than we think. If you want to see for yourself, look at a book on interior design and notice how much attention they pay to the topic. You could even try a little experiment of your own: try writing 'hot!', or 'danger!' with a green marker and try writing 'go!' in red. In other words try to combine 'opposites' in the same image. You will see how odd it looks – indeed, some people react very strongly to paradoxical image like this, so be careful if you try them out on your friends.

But over and above the party tricks, there is a serious point here for anyone who prepares their own support materials.

■ *Avoiding interference*

If you inadvertently create an image which distracts the audience, then that image is competing with your message rather than supporting it; it will interfere with the communication process. There are many causes of distraction, some of which we have already examined, but others include: spelling mistakes, untidiness (flip charts written by a doctor, for example), using symbols which the audience do not understand, using diagrams which are unfamiliar to them. Also, in some circumstances, support material which looks too slick can generate the wrong response from an audience. As ever, the most important thing is that the support material should be appropriate to the audience's expectations and to the nature of the talk.

■ *Highlight the main point*

Make sure that the point you are trying to highlight in your talk stands out clearly in the support material. For example, if, during your talk about the motor car, you want to show people where the oil dipstick is, there is no point in showing them a slide of the general scene under the bonnet. The dipstick will be lost in the million and one things that make up the gubbins around the engine. You must draw the audience's attention to the dipstick by making it stand out from its surroundings. But how?

Perhaps you should not use a slide at all. Perhaps a picture, any picture, will necessarily contain too much detail. So the answer may be to use a diagram or a sketch instead. On the other hand, if it is important that the audience sees the real thing, then by all means use a slide or a photograph, but plan it out first. Should it be in colour or in black and white? What is the best angle for the shot? Should you use two pictures – one to orientate the audience ('Here we are looking at the left hand side of the engine – notice the red cables near the middle of the picture') and the other (close up) to show the actual location of the dipstick. ('There, in the middle of the shot, just below the red cables, you can see the dipstick.')

5-1   Creating contrast by toning down, see the next page.

Firstly, the audience is very seldom interested in all the figures. At most they are interested in totals and sometimes they are interested only in the conclusions you have drawn from them. Secondly, the figures are boring and, for some people, confusing. Thirdly, your support materials should have impact - that is how they support your words.

Too much information is like a snowstorm; there are too many individual flakes to make any sense, in fact, there are so many that they tend to 'white out' the scenery. You should be using a few snowballs to get your points across; they will have much more effect.

Ideally you should not try to present more than two or three main points with any one item of support material.

■ Size

Make sure that the information you present is big enough to be seen clearly by everyone in the audience.

You can pick out the essential details in a number of ways – and this goes for OHP transparencies as well as slides. For example you could tone down the image except for the important detail – i.e. create contrast in the image, *not* by highlighting the main item, but by darkening all the rest. This is what I have done in Figure 5-1. Another way is to superimpose an arrow on the image to point to the important detail. Here is another way of bringing out the key point from that same piece of text.

5-2   Directing the audience's attention to a specific point.

Firstly, the audience is very seldom interested in all the figures. At most they are interested in totals and sometimes they are interested only in the conclusions you have drawn from them. Secondly, the figures are boring and, for some people, confusing. Thirdly, your support materials should have impact - that is how they support your words.

Too much information is like a snowstorm; there are too many individual flakes to make any sense, in fact, there are so many that they tend to 'white out' the scenery. You should be using a few snowballs to get your points across; they will have much more effect.

Ideally you should not try to present more than two or three main points with any one item of support material.

■ Size

Make sure that the information you present is big enough to be seen clearly by everyone in the audience. This is another reason for not presenting too much information in one go.

Use layout as part of the message

In cultures where people read things from left to right and from the top of the page downward, they also seem to interpret priorities in the same sequence. We assume that the first item in a list is the most important item. And we assume that when there are several columns of information on a page, the first column on the left is the most important one. It pays to remember this when you are designing your support materials.

You can also use this effect positively to provide unspoken prompts to the audience. Let us take the example of a simple written support 'visual' such as you might display on a flip chart, or blackboard.

If you want to reinforce the point that the thing you are describing has three major elements, each of which has sub-elements, you might use a layout such as the one I have shown here.

```
  POWER TO WHEELS            Power to wheels

  * ENGINE                   Engine
    Crankshaft               Crankshaft
    Flywheel                 Flywheel

  * CLUTCH                   Clutch
    Friction Plate           Friction plate
    Thrust bearing           Thrust bearing

  * GEARBOX                  Gearbox
```

In the illustration on the left I have arranged the image so the more important points are to the left of and above the less important items. The audience will interpret that message without the need for you to say anything. They will see which components are subordinate to which major element.

On this visual there is very little information, but it is enough to make the point. The three major headings will organise the information and make it less intimidating. I have also used capital letters to signify the relative importance of the items listed and I have used asterisks as 'bullet points' to guide the eye.

The audience will remember the information because the first chart echoes the relationships within the information itself. Spacing and layout, in addition to the use of capitals and lower case, are the only tools I have used to create the visual pattern. Notice how much 'white space' there is on the chart.

It is not a waste of paper, it plays a vital part in helping the audience sort and interpret the message.

In the second chart, on the right, I have not used layout and white space to do specific jobs. Instead, I have done what many presenters do: simply list the items I am going to cover. The chart contains the same information, but it is very difficult to discern its shape and so it is far less effective in supporting the talk. It might even compete with the speaker's words, because the audience may be tempted to waste time trying to work out what the visual is saying rather than listening. The audience will find the visual less memorable – let's not beat about the bush: it's boring, and probably best forgotten anyway.

USING THE MATERIAL

Preparing effective support material is not enough on its own. You also need to think about when and how to use it.

■ Know when to use the material

There are a number of pitfalls to be avoided here. I've listed the main ones below.

■ *Hand-outs*

If you decide to hand out a printed document to reinforce the point you are making, make the point first and then hand out the support document. If you hand it out before you make the point, people will concentrate on the document rather than on what you are saying. Sometimes you will have to use a hand-out first because it contains the point you are going to make. On these occasions, make sure that you highlight the point in some way *before* you hand out the document: perhaps circle the point in red, or tone down the parts of the document which are not relevant to the point.

■ *Slides and films*

If you have to use a slide show, film strip or film – i.e. any medium which needs a darkened room – do not use it immediately after lunch. The sound track will be drowned out by snores if you do. If I use these media at all, I only do so with great reluctance; as a last resort. The fact that the room is darkened means that I am breaking my contact with the audience. I cannot see their reactions, so I am unable to monitor what is happening to my presentation.

If you have to use moving pictures to make your point, try video instead of film. If you want to show still pictures or photographs, try using the OHP (overhead projector), or try handing out copies of the photographs. Use media which allow you to work in natural light, so you can still see the audience.

- *Prepared agendas*

If you are trying to create the impression that your audience is setting the agenda for your talk, do not display a prepared agenda at any time. You may know in advance what the audience likely to say and it is quite pleasing to find that you are right, but keep that knowledge to yourself. There is a temptation to say 'I thought you would come up with that list, so I prepared this one earlier.' Fight the temptation. Nobody likes a smart alec!

- *Too much too soon*

If the topic you are describing is complex, support materials can help the audience make sense of it, but it is sometimes a mistake to reveal too much of the information in one go. It may be much better to build up the picture in several steps, each one adding to the previous illustration. For example, if you are describing the layout of a factory or a house, perhaps step one would be to draw a plan of the main walls. In step two, you could fill in the dividing walls on the ground floor. Then you might add the details for the entrance hall, and so on, until you end up with a detailed drawing which the audience will be able to interpret more easily. The final picture may be very complex indeed, but they will be able to cope with it, simply because they have seen it grow before their eyes. They will be able to interpret the detail because they are aware of the underlying structure

Make sure that everyone can see the material

There is little point in producing top-class support materials for your talk unless every member of the audience can see them clearly. If you are giving your talk in a room which has pillars, or if the audience are seated one behind the other, make sure that you position the support material where it can be seen by everyone. If this is not possible, then make the support material mobile so you can move it around the room. In the worst situation you may have to arrange things so everyone is issued with their own copy of the support material.

This is less than satisfactory, because you have so little control over the audience's use of the support material. It is important that the audience sees the right material at the right time. If the audience are looking at the wrong item, it may create the same effect as seeing the MGM lion and hearing it bark. Bad timing can be like hearing the shot before the villain pulls the trigger.

And here are a few more practical points you should try to remember.

■ *Sitting at a desk*

If you are having a meeting across a desk (back to the bank manager) and you want to use documents as support materials, either have one copy of the documents for yourself and one for each member of the audience, or place the documents so they are the right way up for the person or people in the audience.

■ *Using an overhead projector*

Try not to put the screen in the centre of the room, because you will either be in someone's way if you stay close, or you will have to keep nipping in and out of view to change the transparencies. Put the screen to one side; the audience's left-hand side if you are right-handed, their right if you are left-handed. That way you can stay near your notes (which you may have pencilled on to the transparency frames) and still give the whole audience a clear view of the images you are presenting.

The OHP was designed to allow presenters to project large images without losing contact with their audience. You should always try to face your audience while you are showing transparencies. There is often a powerful temptation to look over your shoulder, just to check the picture is actually there behind you; resist it.

If you have to set up the projector with the audience in the room, don't leave anything to chance. Try to get into the room while it is still empty and have a 'dry run'. Set up the projector so you can get a crisp focus on the projected image. This will tell you two things: firstly it will give you a rough idea of how far away from the screen you will have to place the projector (which will make it easier to set up while the audience is watching you – particularly if you mark its position on the desk with a couple of strips of masking tape). And secondly, it will tell you if you will be able to get a square picture on the screen.

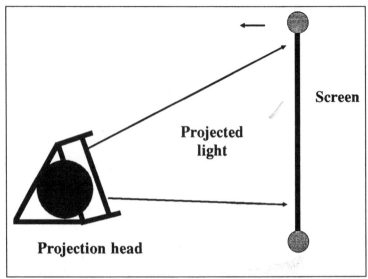

5-3   Simplified diagram of OHP and screen, seen from the side.

If the screen is not parallel to the projection head you will get a distorted image (see Figure 5-3). The projected light leaving the top of the projection head has to travel further than the light at the bottom. Consequently, as the rays of light are diverging, the light at the bottom of the projected image 'spreads apart' less than the light at the top. The result is a picture which is narrower at the bottom than it is at the top – the so called 'keystone effect'. This result is not only aesthetically annoying, but worse than this, you can never have all of the picture in focus at the same time. If you focus the top of the picture, the bottom will be slightly out of focus and vice versa. If you focus the middle of the picture, both the top and bottom will be out of focus. Nine times out of ten, this is more of an irritation than a real problem, but if you want to project, for example, some finely detailed architectural drawings, then the position is quite different. The solution is to find a way of tilting the top of the screen in the direction of the arrow in Figure 5-3, or perhaps having some photocopies made and distributing them instead.

Always check that you have a replacement bulb for the OHP. They don't blow very often, but you can guarantee that, when they do go, it will be at the worst possible time.

When you set up the OHP with the audience in the room, line it up with the masking tape markers, plug it in and switch on. Your first job is to focus the image. Do not use one of the transparencies you intend to use during your talk – you will destroy its impact when you come to use it. Instead, take a coin (50p if you can run to it) and place it in the middle of the big square 'Fresnel lens' (where you put the transparencies when you want to project them). Align and focus the projection head, so the 50p appears black and sharp in the middle of the viewing screen. This bit of arcane trickery impresses people no end. It also gives you time to settle down, so take your time.

Clear a space on either side of the OHP. If you are standing to the left of the machine, place your unused transparencies, in the correct sequence, in the left hand space. As you use the transparencies, place them *face down* in the space on the right. That way you will keep them in the right sequence.

■ *Using a flip chart, white board, or blackboard*

If you are using a flip chart or a marker board of some kind on an easel, again, place it to one side of the 'stage' (preferably at the rear – furthest away from the audience – so you don't trip over it when you have a burst of enthusiasm).

Consider using two flip charts, one at either side of the stage. Use the one on the left for your main headings and use the one on the right to explore details which flow from to the main headings. The advantage of this approach is that the audience have a constant reminder of the structure of your presentation and at the same time, you have the freedom to extemporise if you have to.

Never write and talk at the same time. It is not only bad manners, but it is very difficult to project your voice to the audience, unless you talk out of the back of your head, which is something not many people would admit to doing. If you are not used to writing with the audience's eyes boring into you, you feel as if the silence goes on forever. Take your time. Stop talking, write down the information, then start talking again. The audience will wait for you. In reality their eyes will not be boring into your back. They will probably welcome the lull. It gives them a chance to shift their position have a scratch, make notes, chat to the person next to them, or any number of other things.

■ *Monitor the conditions in the room*

You may have taken all the precautions I've listed, but you may have had to take them several hours before you stand up to speak, so the conditions will have changed. For example, if your screen, or flip chart, or marker board is near a window, and it is a sunny day, make sure that as the sun moves around, the light from the window does not swamp the images you are displaying.

If it is a hot day, and the window is open, put something on your carefully arranged hand-outs to stop them blowing away. In short, keep your wits about you at all times.

You will need support materials for all your talks. Remember that *you* are your most adaptable aid. You can stress points with gestures, with expressions, with posture and with silence. But you have a wide range of other devices which you can use to bring your topic to life for the audience. Always be clear about why you are using your support materials – they must have a specific purpose. Make sure that they can fulfil their purpose by getting the timing right and by making sure that the audience can see them clearly.

The nature of the audience determines whether a particular aid is the right one or the wrong one for the job in hand.

6 Starting your talk

Whether you are talking to one person or to a group, your responsibility actually starts long before the 'audience' gathers together. It is up to you to ensure that everything goes smoothly, so you will be busy for some time beforehand. When you do begin to speak, you should make a positive start, preferably bang on time!

The first part of the checklist tells you how to get a *group* presentation started in a professional way. It is in such situations that you, the presenter, have most responsibility, but many of the points also apply in one way or another to much less formal presentations.

I have tried to list the items most commonly required. However, it is unlikely that every item on the list will apply to every talk you give, so ignore any which are not relevant.

Starting your talk

Checklist

Before the presentation

☐ Check location of power points and extension leads

☐ Check that all equipment works and that there are no trailing leads or other hazards

☐ Get spare bulbs, pens, pads, chalk, etc

☐ Arrange seating

☐ Check that presentation notes are to hand

☐ Check that samples, diagrams and hand-outs are available

☐ Check location of fire exits and toilets

☐ Check lunch/coffee/tea arrangements

☐ Make final preparations

First impressions

☐ Take control from the outset

☐ Establish contact with the group (immediately)

☐ Go through your opening ritual

☐ Project a confident image

BEFORE THE PRESENTATION

■ Check location of power points and extension leads

It is a law of nature that power points are located to suit the needs of electricians rather than the requirements of anyone wanting to use the room. Almost certainly there will either not be enough power points, or they will be in the wrong place. Always check. If you cannot go to see for yourself, make sure you get a sketched plan of the room with the power points marked in. It is usually a good idea to have a four-way extension lead in your 'kit' just in case. The mere fact that a power point exists does not guarantee that it will work, and you may have to use one which is in a less than convenient position.

■ Check that all equipment works and that there are no trailing leads or other hazards

Personally, I do not like to rely too heavily on electrical equipment. I try to design my presentations to be as simple as possible. When I have no alternative but to structure my sessions around particular pieces of equipment I always have a contingency plan for what to do when the equipment fails. For example, if I am using an overhead projector, I make sure that I also have a flip chart, or some printed hand-outs just in case. With something as critical as video, where there is no real alternative, I try to have two sets of equipment available on site. Failing that, I make sure that I have the telephone number of an engineer who will provide a rapid emergency service while I fill in with something else.

If you are going to use electrical or electronic equipment, it pays to know something about the machine – after all, your reputation may suffer if it fails. With slide projectors or overhead projectors, make sure that you know how to change a bulb and remember they get *very* hot. In any case, you should never touch the bulb with your fingers, because you will leave a greasy fingerprint which causes the bulb to blow even more quickly. If you use a clean handkerchief, you can change the bulb safely if you have to.

Modern electronics are generally very reliable. If something does go wrong it is usually something mechanical rather than electronic – such as a plug, or a cable, or a switch. Get to know the connections, and check that they are firm and secure. Test every piece of equipment *on site* before your presentation. If it goes wrong and your presentation collapses about your ears, standing there wailing 'It worked in the office this morning' does not help the situation a great deal.

If you decide to use a piece of equipment which has to be located at a distance from the power point, make sure that no one (particularly you) can trip over the lead. Tape it to the floor, or cover it with a piece of carpet or cardboard. If all else fails, put something bulky (such as a chair) astride the cable so people have to walk around it.

▆ Get spare bulbs, pens, pads, chalk, etc

If you are going to use a flip chart or a marker board, make sure that all the marker pens work. If you find one that does not work readily, throw it into the bin straightaway – that way you are unlikely to pick it up by mistake when you are in full flow. Make sure that the flip chart pad has enough blank sheets left for your session. If you are using a blackboard, or a marker board, make sure you have a board rubber that works. And don't forget that if you are going to use a blackboard, you will need chalk.

Always carry a supply of spares in your emergency kit, including any or all of the following: spare bulbs and fuses, an electrical screwdriver and at least one size of cross-head screwdriver, pens and pencils, masking tape and scissors, magic markers, chalk, flip chart pad, blank overhead projector (OHP) transparencies, spirit-based markers for the OHP transparencies, a ruler, notepads, blank name cards, paper clips, bulldog clips, a clock or watch and a long piece of string. Or you could take one of those all–purpose army pen-knives.

▆ Arrange the seating

The way you arrange the seating can modify the atmosphere for your talk. Of course, if you are speaking in someone else's office, or in a lecture theatre, or if you are just one speaker at a large gathering, you will have no control over seating. But even here, if you understand what the seating plan 'says' to the audience, you can use that knowledge for your own ends. The first thing to realise is that seating *can* have an effect.

It varies from audience to audience and from topic to topic, but broadly speaking, if you want to create a friendly, open atmosphere, with lots of interchange, then members of the audience should be able to see each other easily. You should arrange them around a central table for a small meeting, or place tables and chairs in a U-shape for a larger meeting. If you want to generate a 'no holds barred' discussion session, then dispense with the tables altogether – a table is a defensive barrier.

With this type of open layout there is a practical limit to the size of group you can cater for; if you try to hold a discussion with much more than about twenty people you will find the whole thing very hard to manage and control. The free and easy atmosphere created by this style of room layout can have its problems, but we shall be discussing how to compensate for them later on.

If you want to address a much larger meeting, or if you want your presentation to be a briefing session, with most of the traffic going from you to the audience (and you have no need or desire for interchange between the members of the audience), then arrange the seats like an old-fashioned classroom. This layout will tend to isolate members of the audience and discourage them from discussing things with other members of the audience.

If you are stuck with a seating plan which cannot be altered easily, then you will have to use other techniques for raising or lowering the 'psychological temperature' during your presentation. We shall also be examining these later (see pages 115–119).

■ Check that presentation notes are to hand.

It is very impressive when a presenter speaks for an hour or so without faltering and without looking at his or her notes. As we have seen, it is also very probably an illusion. The vast majority of speakers need a memory jogger of some kind. The trick lies in disguising the fact. Politicians and TV presenters use an 'auto-cue machine' but that might be a bit out of place at the firm's annual dinner.

For most talks, there is actually no need to hide the fact that you are using notes; the audience regards them as being completely natural. We have already discussed how to prepare, use and disguise notes. Now you simply need to check that you remembered to bring them.

Check that samples, diagrams and hand-outs are available

Most presentations benefit from the inclusion of 'props' of some kind. If we want people to remember what we say, then we have to give them some assistance; we discussed why, how and when to use support materials in the previous chapter. *Well before* the session is due to start, make sure you have your support materials with you. If you have forgotten any, this will give you time to create new ones. *Just* before you are due to start, check that they are in the right sequence and that they are clearly numbered.

Check location of fire exits and toilets

If yours is going to be a lengthy presentation in a room which is unfamiliar to the audience, then they will appreciate it if you tell them where the toilets are. They can then relax until they need them. Also you can avoid the distraction of having to find out where they are and then giving directions during your talk. It looks more professional if you take the trouble to think of details such as this.

In the event of a fire, the group will look to you to tell them what to do, so make sure that you *know* what to do and where to go. Don't waste time checking if the alarm is genuine, or if it is simply a fire-drill. Give the group firm and clear instructions and react immediately. If the alarm was just a drill, or if it was false, you will soon know. It is better to waste a bit of time than to be responsible for putting the lives of your group at risk.

The shared experience of a fire drill, a false alarm, or perhaps a genuine problem (such as a real fire and a real bomb threat), brings the group closer together; they have a common point of contact. As a result, the atmosphere in the room *after* the event is always quite different from the atmosphere before; it is more relaxed, more co-operative; unified. In short, a much better working environment.

Check lunch/coffee/tea arrangements

If you are going to speak for some time and you are to pace your session properly, you need to know the times when you can expect interruptions. There is nothing more annoying and deflating than to build your presentation to a gradual crescendo, carrying your audience with you every step of the way, only to find a waiter bursting in with a clattering tea trolley just as you reach the major point. It is as bad as someone saying the punchline of your joke just as you take the breath to say it yourself.

Once you know the timetable, you can build your presentation around the breaks, making key points just *before* you are due for an interruption. Watch out for the lunch break in particular; the half hour or so after lunch is the worst time to get your points across.

If you are just one of many participants in a day-long session and you find that you have been allocated the first session after lunch, do everything you can to get your presentation rescheduled: make excuses, stamp your foot, say you have a peptic ulcer, say you have to be home early to pick the children up from school, anything short of breaking the law or looking foolish. If all these tactics fail, be prepared to start your presentation with a bang. I don't mean that you should shoot yourself – things are rarely that bad – but I do mean that you should have some stratagem for shaking people out of their post-lunch torpor.

On the other hand, if you are running a presentation which lasts for the whole day, then you will have to know when and where the lunch will be served so you can be sure your audience gets to the right place at the right time. Try to arrange for the audience to work on a task of some kind immediately after lunch, preferably in groups (the arguments will wake them up). When they are alert and awake again, then step in and carry on with your contribution.

Make your final preparations

Don't leave things to chance and don't leave things to other people; they are not the ones whose credibility will suffer if something silly goes wrong. Be prepared for the worst. It might never happen, but then you don't wear a lifejacket because you *expect* to be shipwrecked.

Being prepared for the worst means having an all-emergencies kit, and it is well worth the effort of putting one together (see the notes near the beginning of this chapter). If at all possible, try to get on site at least half an hour before the audience to allow yourself time to check all the arrangements and equipment, and to rearrange the seating if necessary. Get the feel of the 'stage' and try to gauge the acoustics of the room so you can judge how forcibly you will have to project your voice. This is easy enough to do if you speak to a colleague who is at the opposite end of the room.

If you are alone, stand at the front of the room and look around. If there are lots of soft drapes and a carpet, they will absorb and deaden the sound in the room, which means you will have to project your voice quite forcefully if you are to be heard clearly by everyone. Clap your hands once, sharply, and listen. If the sound is dull and there are no echoes, this confirms that the room has a 'dead' acoustic. If you hear a brittle echoing sound, then it has a 'bright' acoustic which requires less effort from you. But remember that when the room fills up, the acoustic will deaden at least slightly.

At first it is difficult to judge how much you need to project when you are talking in a room with a dead acoustic, it is surprising how hard you have to work to 'fill the room'. Don't talk to the people in the back row, because the sound of your voice will probably fall short. Instead, imagine someone standing on the other side of the back wall with their ear pressed against it, and talk to *them*. It is like the old boxer's maxim, 'If you want to hit hard, don't aim for the chin, aim eighteen inches beyond it.'

Get yourself settled and comfortable before the audience starts to arrive. Put your notes, hand-outs and props within easy reach, in places where you can find them when you need them.

You should have a list of the people who are due to attend. If your presentation is to a relatively small number (up to, say, twenty people) greet them individually as they arrive and shake each one by the hand; the human contact will make them (and you) feel more relaxed. You can also use this as an opportunity to get used to talking in the room as its acoustics change (remember, as the room fills up the acoustics will 'deaden').

If you want the session to be relatively informal, it is often a good idea to get each member of the audience to fill in a name card which they can prop up at the front of their table or desk. This gives them something to do when they arrive, enables you to tick the names of people who have arrived and saves you from having to remember every single name – always assuming you *have* remembered to bring your specs.

Try to start your presentation precisely on time. If two or three members of the audience still have not arrived you may decide to give them five more minutes. But *always* announce your intentions to the people who *have* arrived; don't keep them waiting without an explanation.

FIRST IMPRESSIONS

Many of the preparations we have been discussing apply only to fairly large audiences. The following hints on how to create the right first impression will be relevant to even the smallest audience.

Take control from the outset

Bearing in mind what we said earlier about nerves, the worst will already be over by now. You established human contact when you greeted the audience. And you will have had a look at the customers and realised that they are just people.

Your talk must have a definite beginning. If you are dealing with a group of people, step forward to the lectern or to a table at the front. The audience will read your signal and they will (usually) end their conversations and settle down to listen. Wait for the silence to fall completely and then make your formal greeting:

'Good morning ladies and gentlemen, Charley Farnsbarns isn't here yet, but we have a lot of ground to cover so I'm afraid we shall have to start without him. If and when he does arrive, I'll brief him on any details he has missed. First, some admin...'

If you are talking to one person, all you need to do is start speaking straightaway. But what about?

The answer is the same for any audience. If you were in their place you would want to know certain things at the outset. Your audience is no different from you in this respect. And it is best for all concerned if you deal with their immediate needs before anything else. If you *don't* deal with their needs they will be nagging away in the background, distracting everyone. And the mere act of running through the information gives you an opportunity to get your voice, throat and breathing up to 'working temperature' while you are still dealing with a relatively neutral topic. More importantly, you will appear businesslike, yet understanding.

There is one other factor which we must not overlook: 'You can take a horse to water, but you can't make him listen to your talk.' You have got to sell yourself and you have to make people *want* to listen to you. You can achieve both these ends by convincing your audience that you are competent, capable and professional – by demonstrating that you are up to the task, *not* by ramming your qualifications and experience down their throats (you might, for all they know, be telling fibs). The best way to impress your audience is by giving them the information they need now. Depending on the circumstances, you might include most, if not all, of the following:

- If they have never met you before they will want to know who you are and why you should be talking to them. (You may like to know that yourself!)

- In some instances they may want to know why *they* are there.

- Rather unflatteringly, one of the things which many people want to know before the session even starts is, what time they can get away.

- For longer sessions, they will want to know the lunch arrangements; whether there are any facilities for people with special dietary needs, the time of the lunch break and the tea and coffee breaks. They will also want to know where lunch will be taken.

- They will want to know where the toilet facilities are and whether a telephone is available.

- Some people will want to know if they can smoke in the room.
- Last, but not least, they will want to know what you expect of them. For instance, do you want them to participate, ask questions, take notes, provide examples from their own experience, buy something, come to a group decision, or perform tasks?

By the time you have worked through these details you will have settled down and your audience will feel more comfortable too.

Establish contact with the audience (immediately)

We have already seen that it is in your interest – and that of the audience – for you to establish human contact from the outset. Eye contact is particularly important. But why?

In normal conversation eye contact plays a much bigger part than people realise. We tend not to notice until we talk to someone who deliberately avoids eye contact, or someone wearing those mirror finish sunglasses. We get an uncomfortable feeling that there is something shifty about the person. Your audience needs eye contact if only to confirm that what you are saying applies to them, so the quicker you establish eye contact evenly throughout the group, the better it is for all concerned, including you, because you will settle down more quickly. But there are more practical reasons as well.

Most human beings are very skilled at monitoring other people's reactions. We do that by watching their faces quite closely and we notice tiny changes which occur in small groups of facial muscles. We can all, for example, tell the difference between a real smile and a false one. Yet, if you analyse the differences you will find they are minute: perhaps only the presence or absence of a slight puffiness in a little pouch below the eyes. Think of the glassy smile of the ballroom dancer and then think how a member of the audience might smile if the dancer's sequinned trousers suddenly fell down around his ankles, and you will see what I mean.

So we are all skilled at reading the signs. But if we do not look at people we will not see the signs. That alone is a powerful reason for establishing eye contact; we can monitor what is happening in the group: 'Why is that chap in the corner grinning to himself? Is it something I've said?' Or, 'Is that glassy stare one of concentration, or is he refusing to accept the point I've just made?' And even, 'Hello, she looks like she wants to ask a question!' We can all read the signs, so I won't go any further.

The moral is, monitor your audience, respond to them quickly, and work with them and through them towards your goal.

The opening ritual

In the chapter about nerves I mentioned that it would help you and your audience if you had a well-rehearsed opening ritual which is the same in structure, but probably not in content, for every presentation you make. One which works for me and which you might like to adapt to your own style is to start each presentation by talking about the Purpose, Benefits and Structure (PBS) of what you are about to say. Do not take that as a fixed sequence. For some topics and some audiences it may be better to have 'Purpose, Structure, Benefits' as your running order. In any case, you might find one running order more comfortable to work with than the others. Choose the sequence you want, but do have an opening ritual for your audience's sake and for your own.

This particular ritual works for any type of verbal communication, whether it be a telephone call, a business meeting, a training session, or a speech on behalf of the bridesmaids.

If you have done your homework properly you will have a carefully prepared plan for your presentation. You will have a good idea of what you are going to say and you will know when you have arrived at the various landmarks along the way. But once again – and not for the last time – put yourself in your audience's shoes. At best they have no idea of where they are going. At worst they may have a totally different idea of what your talk is going to be about.

Your presentation should not be a mystery tour; if it is, your audience may be unwilling passengers, but you want passengers who will get out and push when the bus gets stuck. In general, the audience will want to help, but they can do so only if they know where they are going. Whether your presentation is one which has been planned for weeks and is due to run for several hours, or a ten-minute presentation to the board at only a moment's notice, your reflex response should be the same.

You need to establish, firstly for yourself, the purpose of the presentation, then one or more reasons why the audience should listen to your message and then the main points of your message. Once you know these things you are in a better position to work toward a clear goal. The same is true for your audience, so start your presentation by telling them too.

As I have said, you can use this procedure (or some other similar formula) at the beginning of every spoken communication, from a phone call to a formal dissertation. The important thing is that the formula remains the same. The amount of time you allot to the activity will depend on the scale of your presentation. For the phone call it may need only three sentences, while for the formal dissertation, you might allow ten minutes or so to deal with these critical points.

If, by chance, any of the audience have quite different expectations of your presentation, then this is the time to sort them out. In most cases, they will come to the presentation with no clear idea of what it's about (even though you took care to send out briefing notes in good time). Once you have told them, it will give them the direction they need to participate fully.

Let's examine the 'PBS' formula in a little more detail. Let me define what I mean by the headings and examine how you go about defining the elements for yourself?

■ *Make the purpose of the presentation clear*

You can make the purpose clear for other people only if it is clear for you. So the first step is to ask yourself, 'Why? Why am I going to make this presentation? Why am I sticking my neck out in front of all these people? There must be a good reason!' It may help you to formulate an answer if we look at some background first.

As far as I can tell, there are really only three reasons for communicating with other people:

- To inform.
- To persuade.
- To entertain.

Every act of communication in any medium has one of these three motives at its heart. Actually, every communication is a mixture of all three, but in differing quantities. So a sales presentation has *persuasion* as its major element, but the salesman has to inform the customer about the merits of his product and he has to be at least a bit entertaining, otherwise the customer will switch off. A project briefing, on the other hand, will be mainly about providing *information*, but it too will have to persuade the members of the project team to co-operate and again it must awaken the listeners' interest and, in a sense, entertain them. The after-dinner speech will probably set out to provide *entertainment*, but it must convey information as well (if only to set up the punchlines) and the speaker has to persuade people to hear him out.

So when you define your purpose, you should begin by asking, what is my *main* task? Is it to inform, persuade, or entertain people about the topic?

Once you have answered the question for yourself, then you can pass on the information to your audience. Except, of course, there may be times when you do not want to betray the true purpose of your presentation:

'Hello lads and lasses. The main purpose of my presentation today is to persuade you that it is a jolly good idea to sack 10 per cent of the people in this room.'

It is not for me to comment on the rights and wrongs of such situations, other than to say that I believe that we should try to be honest at all times. Even so, there are ways and ways of saying things, so perhaps I have been guilty of disguising my intentions on occasions. But none of this reduces the audience's need to know the purpose of your presentation, so if you don't feel able to give them the real purpose, give them one which is quite close to the real one – and make sure that it is a plausible:

'Hello everyone. You all know things have been very tight during the last year. I want to tell you about what has been happening to the company and what our prospects are for the coming year.'

Give the audience a reason for listening

We saw earlier that the audience and the presenter have their allotted roles – the presenter talks and the audience is expected to listen. But that does not mean that the audience *wants* to listen, any more than it means that you want to talk. You may have been persuaded or coerced into giving a presentation, but you cannot coerce an audience. You have to make them want to listen, so you have to sell yourself (as we have already seen) and your presentation.

If you are to sell anything to anyone you have to persuade them that it will definitely benefit them personally: *this* washing powder will make you a better mum, *that* beer will make you smarter than all the other dullards in the pub, the other soft drink will make you sweat in a more macho way. Whatever the benefit, it must be seen as a personal benefit to the buyer. In this instance 'the buyer' is the individual member or members of your audience. But all too often organisational changes, for example, are sold on the basis that they will be good for the company: 'The new XYZ computer will make the company more efficient and thus more profitable.'

The implied benefit in this statement is that increased profits mean greater job security and higher wages for us all. But many people will find it difficult to make that connection. For them the benefit is not so much implied as buried. On the other hand some people's reaction to the statement will be the exact opposite of what was intended: 'Why should I want to make someone else even richer!' So a vague statement such as this will not work reliably because it is not targeted to the audience's perception of personal benefits.

Choosing which benefit to stress depends very much on precise circumstances, but the key point is that each member of the audience must perceive the benefit as being a tangible one for them. Something along these lines might be nearer the mark: 'The new XYZ computer will take all the drudgery out of your work.'

Even this is open to criticism, though. To some people, one man's drudgery is another man's comforting routine. Others in the firm may suspect that the XYZ computer will in fact take all their work out of the drudgery. You have to know what makes your audience tick and you need to give them a sound reason for listening. It is often difficult to come up with a snappy answer. Perhaps the only way is to put yourself in their position and ask: 'Why would I want to hear about this topic?'

■ *Explain the structure of the presentation*

This is where you tell your audience about the major stages in their journey through the topic with you: 'First we shall look at this, then we shall see that and ultimately we shall ....' Some examples will illustrate the point.

'In today's session we shall start by looking at the historical background, then we can examine the position today and finally we can go on to make some informed guesses as to what might happen in the future. First, the historical background ...'

'We have a full programme ahead of us today ladies and gentlemen. In a few moments I shall get the ball rolling by running through a short review of the underlying theory. Then we can split into working parties and deal with a range of case studies for the major part of the day. At about four o'clock we shall re-convene to hear the reports of each of the working parties. You all have colour-coded cards in front of you as well as a key chart which tells you where each working party will be located.

The coloured tab at the top right of the card tells you which working party you are to join. Are there any questions? [pause] Very well. The underlying theory ...'

'In our working party we discerned three major trends which have a bearing on this. I should like to talk about each of the three in turn and then finish off with the general conclusions which we have drawn from our analysis of those trends. The most obvious trend ...'

There is an old trainer's maxim which fits here rather well. When you are making a presentation, 'First, tell 'em what you're gonna tell 'em. Then tell 'em. Then tell 'em what you've told 'em.' There is more than a grain of good advice in that maxim.

The three examples above illustrate the first element in the maxim and the third element of our opening ritual. They show how a quite uncomplicated statement can put people's minds at rest. In fact, that is the whole point of the opening ritual itself. It settles people down by giving them their bearings. When you have finished the ritual they will know why they are there, how they will benefit, and what to expect during the talk.

Let me repeat – I have suggested that your ritual should be Purpose, Benefits, Structure (PBS), but do not take that as a fixed sequence. For you, it may be better to have Purpose, Structure, Benefits as your running order. Choose the sequence you want, but *do* have an opening ritual for your audience's sake and for your own.

Here are some examples to show you how the same basic formula, PBS or a variant, might be employed in three very different types of verbal presentation.

The first example is a tele-sales call to a famous explorer:

'Hello, is that Mr Livingstone, I presume? I'd like to tell you about a place which even you may not have visited [plausible purpose]. You might be interested in being one of the first, if not *the* first, people to go to this tropical paradise [benefit]. I'd like to tell you where it is, how to get there and give you details of flights and bookings [structure].'

Here is a more sober example:

'Ladies and gentlemen, last week there was a series of accidents in the mixing plant which held up production for three days. Fortunately, nobody was hurt, but we did, all of us, lose our productivity bonus as a direct result. It is my task, today, to report on the investigation which my department have been carrying out [purpose]. We can all learn from the events of last week and we can take steps to see that it never happens again [benefits].

I want to begin by drawing up a plan of the mixing plant, then I want to describe precisely how the accident was triggered and how its effects spread. Finally I shall put forward a set of recommendations which we believe will eliminate all chances of it happening again [structure].'

Finally we have the introduction to a course called 'Successful Presentations':

'All of us here are naturally quite expert at verbal communication. We all have our own store of skills, but some people are more skilled at certain things than others, so it is my job during the next three days to put forward some ideas and to channel *your* ideas and experience so we can all sharpen up our presentation skills [purpose].

Courses like this – especially with the video camera leering at you – will put you under more pressure than you will find in real life, but at the same time, if you try out a new technique and it fails, you have lost nothing, because we can examine what happened and see why it failed for you. It could be that a particular technique is not for you, but you will never know unless you try it. It is usual for people who come on the course to make distinct and noticeable improvements and there is usually at least one person on each course who makes a startling improvement [benefits].

You will find that this is a very practical course – you will be doing all the work! We shall start each day with a formal presentation, in which I shall cover the theory behind what we are doing. For the rest of the day you will be applying the techniques discussed in my presentation. You will be making four presentations in total. And we'll be using the video equipment to record your presentations, so you can see for yourself how you are performing. So the pattern for each day will be the same: a presentation from me for an hour or so, then for the rest of the day you will be preparing and making a presentation – with feedback from the rest of the group – and from me [structure].'

For longer sessions, say, anything more than thirty minutes, you should go through the opening ritual not only at the very beginning of the talk, but also at the start of each major phase. The opening ritual will orientate the audience for the whole session, while the ritual at the start of a new phase will orientate them for the phase they are about to start. These 'in-journey briefings' should cover the purpose and the structure of the next stage, but you may decide that a statement of benefits at every stage is not so essential.

Project a confident image

In a sense this final point is superfluous. If you have done everything on the checklist then you have no reason for not feeling confident. Even if you're not overflowing with confidence, at least you won't be projecting the image of someone who feels threatened. The main thing is that – having read all the signals of your businesslike manner – your audience will feel they can have confidence in you.

In conclusion, make sure that everything is set up and working well before the start of your presentation, check that you have everything you need, then step up and take control. Go through your opening ritual, settle down and maintain the impetus. Once you get started, monitor the reactions of your audience to make sure that they, and you, are on course.

7 Using your voice

Your voice is just one of the tools available to you, but it is by far the most important one. You can do a number of things to ensure that you use your voice to the full and that is what we shall be examining in this chapter.

Any actor will tell you that the voice is the most wonderfully versatile medium of expression – Peter Sellers used to create his characters starting from the voice and building outward. Think of famous voices like those of Winston Churchill, Richard Burton, Orson Welles, or Bugs Bunny. You have the same tool available to you, but you may never have been shown how to use it. If that is so, we can start now.

But first let me say that I do not pretend to be a speech therapist. This is very much first aid, rather than full treatment. If you have serious problems with your speech, you should see your doctor.

Using your voice

Checklist

Voice control

☐ Control your breathing

☐ Project, don't shout

☐ Vary the pitch, tone and volume

☐ Don't swallow the ends of words and sentences

Speaking techniques

☐ Use pauses for punctuation

☐ Use questions

VOICE CONTROL

■ **Control your breathing**

As we have already seen, you need to control your breathing so you can calm yourself down and control your adrenalin. Once you are into the talk proper, even after you have calmed down, you will still need to breathe in a particular way – simply because you are talking. The chances are that you will do this naturally and you won't even have to think about it, but about 10 per cent of the people who read this book will need to take conscious action. If you are in that 10 per cent who run out of breath halfway through a sentence, or gabble your words, running one sentence into the next, these next few paragraphs are for you.

In normal conversation our sentences tend to be quite short because we share the 'air time' with the other person or people involved in the conversation. It is normally only when we are telling a story, or a long joke that we speak more than a couple of sentences at a time. You will know from your own experience that a conversation is like a tennis match, with a serve and a return of serve, sometimes followed by a short rally. When you are speaking more formally the situation is quite different. Quite often there is no interplay at all and even when there is interplay it is usually much more sporadic.

Normal shallow breathing is fine for conversation which requires only relatively short bursts of fairly low energy. However, the formal situation calls for much longer bursts of energy and if you are talking to a number of people in a large room then those longer bursts also have to be of higher energy – simply to fill the room. The energy is supplied by your breath, so your normal breathing pattern will not do. You will not be able to deliver the energy you need. It is like the difference between a polite cough and a real hack: you can cough discreetly without breathing in at all, but if you want to clear a troublesome frog in the throat, then you have to take a deep breath first.

When you are speaking more formally you will also have to slow down your normal rate of speech and to pronounce your words clearly. Breathing more deeply will automatically cause you to slow down and will help with your pronunciation. Let me be

---

precise here, I am not suggesting that you should change your normal accent, or your pronunciation, simply that you should take a little more care to pronounce things clearly so people can hear you even at the back of the room.

Increased adrenalin causes our muscles to tighten up, and that includes our throat muscles. This is why our voices rise in pitch when we feel under stress. We have already seen that deeper breathing will help us relax and counter the 'Minnie Mouse' syndrome, but we need to do more than this; hence the next step in the checklist.

Project, don't shout

If you are talking in a large room with lots of soft, sound-absorbing surfaces, such as curtains and carpets and people, it becomes very hard to fill the room with your voice so everyone can hear clearly. You therefore find yourself having to 'pump up the volume'.

If you are already feeling the stress, or if your natural voice already has quite a high pitch, then pumping up the volume by simply shouting will cause the vocal cords to work that much harder. This has two effects: firstly you may end up with a sore throat and secondly you will probably sound like a demented banshee. Your voice will take on an unpleasant hectoring and strident edge which will work against you.

Yet the fact remains that you have to fill the room with your voice, so how do you do it without bursting a blood vessel and destroying your image?

The answer is to *project* your words rather than to shout them. We have seen that the power source for our speaking gear is our lungs – or, more accurately, the breath in our lungs. And we know that we make sounds by expelling the air from our lungs through the vocal cords. We then modify the basic sound by changing the shape of the mouth and tongue. In other words, we use the mouth and tongue to control the shape of the sound, while we control the pitch by tightening and loosening the vocal cords.

There is one further element to consider. The basic sound we produce has to be amplified to make it audible to others. Most of us (certainly most English people) rely on natural resonating chambers in our heads to provide the amplification, which is fine for normal face to face conversation, but in a large or acoustically 'dead' room this is sometimes not enough.

Faced with the need to increase volume, our immediate reaction is simply to expel air through the vocal cords more forcibly, i.e. shout. But doing this uses only one of the voice controls available to you. Remember, four physical elements control the sound that comes out of your mouth: your breath, your vocal cords, the shape of your mouth and your resonating chambers. Two of these control the 'loudness': the amount and speed of the breath and the resonating chambers. It seems sensible that if you have a set of controls, you should use them all.

Of course, if you want to increase the volume for a short time and you are not concerned about the timbre of your voice, by all means go ahead and shout, 'Help!' or 'Look out!' or 'Stop that this instant!' But if you want to sustain a high volume level for some time and you don't want to sound grating and neurotic, then use all four controls available to you. Firstly, keep your vocal cords relaxed. In fact, you should consciously relax your throat, neck and shoulder muscles. Secondly, when you are speaking, open your mouth more widely than you would in normal conversation.

That leaves two of your controls - the resonating chamber and the power source. You will need to make some other adjustments to them, but these are more difficult to describe. Generally people say something like 'push from your diaphragm while you speak', but I am not sure how intelligible this piece of advice is.

You may find it easier to interpret if you try a couple of simple exercises. (The following few paragraphs are by no means a technical description of how to project; all I want to do is point you in the right direction. You will need to practise the technique on your own.) Imagine yourself talking to a friend who is only a couple of feet away from you. Say 'Mary had a little lamb' out loud and try to feel where your voice is vibrating. For many English people the vibrations will seem to be somewhere near the top of the throat. Now hold your nose and repeat the exercise. If you produce a sound like 'Bary had a diddle dam', then your voice is what we can call a 'top of the throat' voice. If holding your nose doesn't seem to make much difference to the sound, there is a good chance that you are already 'vibrating' in the right place. (For many Scots, Welsh and American speakers the voice seems to come from much further back, because they naturally vibrate in the right part of the throat.)

Try holding your nose and saying 'Mary had a little lamb' in an American accent and you may see what I mean. Alternatively, try speaking like 'Medallion Man' (you know, the brash smoothie with the Elvis Presley curled lip and the half-closed Robert Mitchum eyes, bursting through the swing doors of the disco saying: 'Hey! Don't you know me from somewhere...?'). When you can hold your nose and say the words without much distortion you will have managed to push your voice further back.

You should feel the vibrations coming from just below your Adam's apple. That is the effect we are looking for, because with the vibrations coming from there, you can now use your *chest* as a resonating chamber rather than your nasal passages. Your chest is much bigger so it will amplify the sound more. Immediately the voice will sound much more powerful and it will drop slightly in pitch. And, because you can get the same volume for much less effort, it will sound less breathy. All in all, the sound will be much warmer and more pleasing. That is the first stage in projecting your voice: getting the vibrations in the right place.

Now we come to the diaphragm bit. Put one hand on your solar plexus, a couple of inches below where your ribs meet, then say 'Mary had a little lamb' in your normal voice and hold the 'Mmm' sound at the end. If you push in on your solar plexus sharply a few times while you are sounding the 'Mmm', you should hear the sound increase in volume, but you might also hear it increase in pitch. Now try the same exercise using your American accent. This time you should hear the sound increase in volume (possibly more so than before) but the pitch should stay roughly the same.

So, you increase the volume by pushing from your solar plexus (your diaphragm). And if you vibrate your voice below your Adam's apple, using your chest as the resonating chamber, you can increase and decrease volume without increasing and decreasing the pitch at the same time. Your voice will sound richer and more interesting. It works wonders on the phone. And you can keep it up for much longer than you could keep shouting.

▄▄▄▄▄▄ Vary the pitch, tone and volume

If you have ever watched a film with subtitles you will know that the human voice can convey much more than just words. Take the words 'Christopher Robin went down with Alice'. You can say those words so that they convey grief, horror, surprise or outrage, as well as many other emotions. Try it for yourself (assuming you aren't reading this on a bus).

If you listen to yourself saying the words in the different ways you will find that you get the effect you want by twiddling three basic controls: pitch, tone and volume. We can all do it to a greater or a lesser extent.

When you are speaking formally, you need to add colour and interest to what you are saying by twiddling these controls. Use your existing skills to add emphasis, to stress particular points, to ask questions, and to convey your feelings about the topic. If you are speaking in a large room you will have to be larger than life. You have to extend your range of pitch and volume, and do it consciously.

It is sometimes difficult to judge how you sound, so try this very old exercise. Get hold of a tape recorder and record yourself reciting a nursery rhyme in your normal voice. Then recite the same rhyme but try to act out the parts. Finally do the same, but this time *over-act*; be melodramatic!

Then play the recordings back and listen to them from the other side of the room. Once you have got over the initial embarrassment you should be able to make a judgement. You will probably find that the first recording sounds dull and flat and monotonous. The second will sound a little less grey, but still not enthralling and the third should sound lively and interesting. It all depends on your normal style of speech. If it already has lots of peaks and troughs then you will not have to act too much, but if it is slightly single-toned, then you may have to try a little harder.

Just remember that your audience will be able to interpret a 'contrasty' picture more easily than one which consists of subtle shades of grey. Also the picture with variety will catch and hold their attention more easily.

Don't swallow the ends of words and sentences

You may not have this fault, but it is a very common habit, particularly when people are feeling a little nervous. You have probably seen it yourself:

'Someone starts a sentence very forcefully but **seems some**how to run out of steam as the sentence progresses.'

There are two problems here: one is purely physical and the other is a lost opportunity. The physical problem is that your audience may simply miss the ends of your words and sentences; they will get lost in the background mush of the transmission ('Did he say forcefully or forcibly? And what was that bit at the end?'). The listeners will persevere for a while, but who can blame them for switching off if they have to do all the work to make sure that your message gets across?

As for the lost opportunity, if you want to stress a particular point, you usually present it at the end of a sentence or at the end of a group of related sentences. For instance, if the key point about a motor car is its economy, you can get the basic information across by saying something like, 'It's cheap to run because it does 50 miles to the gallon on two-star fuel.' The bit which stands out is that it runs on two-star fuel, but that is not the complete point you are trying to make. If you change the sequence of the ideas and at the same time increase the volume slightly at the end, the effect will be quite different. You might say, 'It does 50 to the gallon on two-star fuel, so it's cheap to run!'

If, on the other hand, you are in the habit of tailing off at the end of sentences, your key points may never get through.

SPEAKING   TECHNIQUES

Use pauses for punctuation

When you are speaking you know more or less what you are
going to say and you know when you have reached the end of one
group of ideas and are starting on a new group. But your
audience does not know. We have a similar problem with writing,
but with the written word there are certain punctuation
conventions which help the reader untangle the ideas: a colon
signifies the start of a list, a comma signifies a small change in the
direction of the ideas. And a full stop says that one idea has
ended and a new one is about to start. A semicolon tells us that
an extra idea has been tacked on to a sentence; as a sort of
afterthought. And a new paragraph marks the end of a group of
related ideas.

You can't use punctuation marks in your talk. Imagine saying:
'Today, comma, I want to talk to you about three things, colon,
space, the first is...' But you can achieve the same *effect* by using
pauses of different lengths, perhaps like this: 'Good morning
ladies and gentlemen. [pause for 3 seconds] For my session, [1 sec] I
want to deal with some typical problems – [½ sec] typical in our
work, that is. [3 secs]'

The audience will be able to interpret the different-length pauses
and they will add shape to the ideas you are expressing. Words in
a constant unbroken stream are featureless, but break them up
with pauses and your audience will be able to follow where you
are leading.

Pauses have another important use. If you're in the habit of
speaking very quickly, your audience may find it difficult to pick
out the separate parts of your talk. There is little point in me
advising you to slow down, because you are going to find it very
hard to change the habits of a lifetime. But if I advise you to use
pauses for punctuation, then you should be able to talk as quickly
as normal between the pauses, but the audience will find it easier
to follow your drift.

Use questions

It may seem odd to cover the topic of questions in a chapter about using your voice, but handling questions is one of the skills you will have to acquire and using questions properly will enhance your verbal presentation.

Many of us shy away from questions. Why is that? I suppose it is because we would prefer, deep down, to stay just a bit distant from the audience; perhaps we feel slightly intimidated by them. But we have already seen that one of the best ways to relax yourself is to make human contact as soon as possible, and questions are a good way to interact with your audience. It is also a good way to get the audience to think about your subject. So let's look at questions in a bit more detail.

The first thing to remember is that questions can work in two directions – if the audience can put pressure on you by asking questions, then you can put pressure on them in the same way. Let us start by looking at questions coming from the audience. Why do people ask questions? There are several possible reasons:

- A genuine request for information, because they have misunderstood something you said earlier, or because they have missed the point entirely, or because you have not made a connection clear to them: 'I don't quite see why...'

- To parade their own mastery of the topic: 'Isn't it true that...'

- To throw a spanner in the works: 'I know you don't want to cover this point, but...'

- To waste time: 'What was it you said about...'

- To state an opinion: 'Wouldn't it be better if...'

- To cast doubt: 'Surely you don't think that...?'

- Not a question at all: 'That's nonsense isn't it!?'

The best way to deal with these 'questions' is to treat them as if they were all genuine requests for information. Innocence is the best form of attack. Stop, consider what the questioner has said and try to establish firstly why he or she has asked the question. If you cannot see how it relates to what you have been saying, or if you suspect that the question may be something other than a request for information, put on your best 'puzzled but willing to help' expression and enquire mildly, 'Er, why are you asking that question? I can't quite see what...'

It is then up to them to justify their position. If it is a genuine request for information, then nobody has lost anything by the few seconds delay. If it isn't a genuine request for information, you will be in a better position to judge what it really is and, therefore, how to deal with it. Here are some hints on how to handle different kinds of questions:

- For the genuine question, provide the answer if you can (if the question is relevant to the objectives you are trying to achieve).

- If the question is designed simply to parade mastery, recognise the questioner's knowledge of the topic. Do not try to top their contribution. Keep them on your side – if they really do know that much, you don't want them on the opposing side.

- If you suspect a spanner-pitching exercise, you need to ask innocent and puzzled-sounding follow-up questions: 'Perhaps I'm being dull, but I don't quite see the point of your question...'

- The time-waster is often as crafty as you are and it is sometimes difficult to tell if he or she is genuinely confused or is confusingly genuine. Try summarising the point in question and then moving on quickly. If all else fails, promise to discuss the point after the talk.

- The way you deal with the opinion-stater depends on the nature of the point you are making. If it is fundamental to your talk, then you might eventually have to agree to differ, but you may lose that person and some others. If you try always to base your talk on facts rather than opinions, this situation is far less likely to occur.

- Dealing with the person who tells you flatly that what you have just said is nonsense is less difficult than it sounds. The immediate reaction is to justify what you have just said – to produce facts and figures to support your case – but this is all a waste of time. All we know for certain is that someone has said 'that's rubbish' or something similar. But what is it that is being 'rubbished'? Is it the point you are making, or the way you were trying to make it? The only thing you can do is to find out more. When you have identified the problem, then you can deal with it. Do not try to down a target until you can see it.

All these variants have one thing in common: they offer you an opportunity to explore the topic, or the group, in more detail. So a question from the floor is a *stepping stone*, rather than a stumbling block. But what about questions from you to the group?

Let us divide them into broad groups first and then we can look at how, when and whether to use them:

- Closed questions – those which can elicit only a 'yes' or 'no', or 'don't know' answer: 'Do you understand?'

- Leading questions – those which carry the expected answer in the question: 'These questions do have their uses, don't they?'

- Open-ended questions – those which generate a reasoned answer. They usually contain at least one of Rudyard Kipling's 'six serving men' – the words what, when, why, who, where, or how: 'How can you answer such a question with a simple "yes" or "no"?'

- Rhetorical questions – those you expect to answer yourself: 'Why use rhetorical questions? Well...'

Each of these has its own uses. If you want to get a quick opinion from someone, use a closed question. If you want to guide someone's responses, use a leading question – though it is a slightly underhand device, so use it carefully. If you want to generate a longer answer or start a discussion, use an open-ended question. As for rhetorical questions, they are one of your most useful tools. I tend to use rhetorical questions a lot, to make the audience consider things they might not have considered before, to construct links between the different sections of my talk and even simply to nudge them into wakefulness.

Rhetorical questions are like a dash of spice and they have the added value of making one-way traffic look two-way.

Dashes of spice are very important. They keep the audience awake, interested and 'entertained'. But don't use rhetorical questions, or indeed any type of question, as your only way to add interest. This whole chapter has been about the ways in which you can make people want to listen to you.

An interesting speaker is one who has something interesting to say, in an interesting way. It is someone who can be heard effortlessly in every corner of the room; whose voice changes in pitch, tone and volume; who uses silence to punctuate paragraphs, sentences and phrases; who involves the audience by posing or responding to questions. In short, someone who makes the audience think about the topic; perhaps in a completely new way.

8 Looking good

This chapter is about your principal presentation aid – you. In some books it might be called something like, 'Avoiding Distracting Mannerisms', or 'Dos And Don'ts' with the emphasis firmly on the don'ts. Here, there is one section which deals with distracting mannerisms, but only one section and even this does not concentrate on what you should not do. Instead it deals with what you could and should do to enhance your talk – the 'mechanics' of talking competently.

We can all recognise what we would loosely call a 'good speaker'. But one good speaker's performance will probably be quite different from another's, yet they must have some things in common. So what do we look for when we assess whether or not a speaker is doing a good job?

If you analyse your own experience you will probably find yourself making fairly broad generalisations, such as: he or she seems very relaxed, very lucid, or on top of the subject matter. We could sum it up most accurately by saying that they seem confident. That is the key; they *seem* confident. That is not to say that they necessarily *are* confident.

If that is what we look for in a speaker, it follows that our audience will be looking for the same thing in us. So how do we project this confident image?

Checklist

☐ Take control and keep it

☐ Manage your mannerisms

☐ Use gestures appropriately

☐ Use facial expressions consciously

☐ Use body language appropriately

☐ Use your position in the room consciously

Take control and keep it

As I have said before, your audience expects you to take control and set the pace. If you do not exhibit firm leadership, you will confuse the audience. Even in one to one situations you will create a better impression if you seem to know what you want and where you are going. It is like the difference between shaking hands with someone who takes a firm and decisive grip and someone who offers you a caress from a wet fish. We get an immediate impression. First impressions count and you only get one chance to create them.

What matters is the impression you create. The audience will not know how many times you have had to go to the lavatory immediately before the talk. They will not know that every so often, without warning, your stomach takes an express lift to your boots. They will not know how little you know about the topic. They will not know the questions you would like to avoid. All they have to go on is the person who steps up to begin the talk. If that person seems diffident and loath to take charge, they will read that as a disappointing weakness. But if that same person strides forward, looks them in the eye, smiles and then starts to lay down the game plan for the talk then they will feel that they can have confidence in the speaker.

One way to project a confident and competent image, without saying a word, is to step forward and make it clear that you will not be rushed, by rearranging things on the desk or the lectern before you start speaking. Like the professional batsman, walk up to the crease, mark out your position, and then stand back to survey the people waiting to catch you out. When you have seen all of them, then signal that you are ready to start by taking your position at the crease. ('Let battle commence!')

That's one way of taking control, but you also need to keep a firm hand on the reins of your talk. You can do that only if you have a clear idea of your purpose and objectives (and it helps to know a bit about the topic). If you are not sure of what you are trying to achieve nor why you are giving the talk, how can you hope to give the clear leadership which the audience needs?

All audiences respect, and often need, leadership, whether they admit it or not. People who are unused to giving formal talks often shy away from what they see as imposing themselves on others. This is particularly true of those who have a good-natured, live-and-let-live approach. They tend to adopt a, 'What I'd *like* to do...' attitude, rather than 'What *we shall* do...'

While the first approach may seem the most democratic, or the least bombastic, it is actually less helpful to the audience than the second. If you really care about people's interests you should provide the leadership and direction they need. After all you are supposed to be the 'expert', so you are expected to know what to do. When you go to the doctor you don't expect him or her to ask you which treatment you want.

Manage your mannerisms

If you analyse how impressionists create a verbal cartoon of a well-known figure, you will see that their impression has several elements, only one of which is the sound of the voice. A television programme like *Spitting Image* works on several levels at the same time. Here, the principal device is the three-dimensional cartoons of the characters, but other factors play a very important part in creating the full picture. The puppets would be lifeless without a voice that often embodies only one recognisable feature; the breathy sound of Sir Robin Day, or the basso profundo tones of Frank Bruno, for example.

Overlaid on these will be certain characteristic gestures, facial expressions and verbal mannerisms ('Know what I mean 'Arry?') So the first point is that our opinion of people is formed not only by what they look like, but also by hearing what they say and noticing how they say it. Every one of us has our own little collection of facial expressions, gestures and mannerisms, which give us a recognisable character. And it is these distinctive features which enable other people to read and interpret what we are saying: the words 'I wouldn't do that if I were you' would have quite different meaning if spoken first by Claire Rayner and then by Big Frank.

So do not try to change your natural style by copying someone else's. In any case, you will find it very difficult to suppress your natural gestures and mannerisms. If someone tells you that they find a certain physical or verbal mannerism distracting, then you may need to do something about it. But take positive action, rather than the negative action of simply trying to stop doing it. Replace the distracting mannerism with something else that seems more natural and is less distracting.

Have you ever wondered why we develop mannerisms; what function they perform for us? I like to think of them as safety valves (what the psychologists call 'displacement activity'); a comforting familiar ritual, like sucking your thumb or holding your blanket. Studies of animals under intensive farming conditions (i.e. under stress) have shown that as, say, overcrowding increases so too does the incidence of certain seemingly meaningless patterns of behaviour, such as pigs biting the bars of their pens, or swaying from side to side. Certainly in public speaking, the more nervous the presenter (i.e. the more they feel under stress) the more likely they are to shift their weight from one foot to the other, click pen tops, scratch various parts of the body, sniff, or jangle keys and loose change in the pocket. Sometimes it gets so bad that you can't hear what the speaker is saying.

But as people get more confident, this random behaviour disappears magically by itself. That is why I believe that it is no help at all to tell people about their twitching and scratching, because it only increases the stress and so makes matters worse. It is far more important that they are sure of what they are trying to do and why they are trying to do it. This knowledge increases confidence, thus reducing unnecessary stress and ultimately cancelling the need for the displacement activity, so it disappears of its own accord.

This is equally true of most mannerisms, but sometimes another factor comes into play as well – laziness. We once had a neighbour whom we used to call Little Mr Whatsisname, because of his verbal mannerism and his physical stature. Standing on tippy toes he would talk to my Irish grandmother over the garden fence, saying something like: 'Scuse me Missis whatsisname, can

I, er, borrow your whatsisname to cut the whatsisname? It's getting a bit... whatsisname and mine's broken.' My grandmother would smile kindly and say 'Of course Alfie dear', then stomp into the house muttering, 'It's time that wee rat bought his own lawnmower!'

It used to annoy my grandmother that Alfie would not take the trouble to use the right names for things – including her. As for Alfie, well I think his problem was partly nerves and partly laziness. My grandmother was enough to intimidate anyone and he was trapped between her and a wife who insisted on having neat lawns, but refused to let him buy a new lawnmower. However, even in more relaxed moments, when he would climb up on to a deckchair to sit in the sun, his conversation was still liberally peppered with whatsisnames because he could not be bothered to hunt around in his head for the right word.

As expressions and set phrases move in and out of fashion we are often tempted to use them because they have a satisfying rhythm or they create a certain buzz for the audience. I have in mind such phrases as 'At the end of the day', or 'The bottom line'. No doubt when expressions such as this were originally coined they had a certain graphic power – both of these examples carry the undertone of 'when the reckoning comes' – but when such phrases are over-used they often lose their original meaning, and indeed, lose all meaning. In the end they often become nothing more than an extended form of 'er...'

As I said earlier, we all have our own mannerisms and most of the time they do not cause any problems; in fact they reflect our characters. But when a characteristic mannerism becomes a distraction, then, as I've said, you may need to do something about it. Remember though, that certain things distract certain people – the mere fact that one person mentions that he found your nose scratching terribly distracting does not necessarily mean that you have a major fault. Ask other people what they think. If there is a general consensus that one of your physical, or, *you know,* verbal mannerisms is, *you know,* distracting, then you may have to, *you know,* do something about it; but only if it is interfering with your ability to communicate. *Know what I mean?*

Use gestures appropriately

I am one of those people who have to use their hands when speaking – strap my arms to my sides and I'm dumb. So, I have never subscribed to the view that the speaker should not use his or her hands. The standard advice used to be: 'Stand with your feet slightly apart with your weight distributed evenly. Clasp your hands lightly together behind your back and keep them there.' When I try to do this I feel like the little boy in the painting, *When Did You Last See Your Father* – and I fairly quickly run out of words. If I can wave my arms about then I feel much more relaxed.

But there is much more to it than simply waving arms about. Gestures have to be appropriate. They must match the words you are using. Try thumping the table and saying 'I really am terribly sorry.' I don't intend to tell you which gestures you should use when, because you already know. But what I will say is that if you are talking to more than a couple of people, you will have to make those gestures larger than life. I don't mean that you should prance about like a ballet dancer, but I do mean that the people at the back of the room should be able to see when you are stressing a point, or illustrating a movement.

The timing of the gestures must also be tightly controlled – they must coincide with the words. There is no point in saying 'It is terribly important!' and then thumping the table half a second later. The thump must coincide with the word you are stressing. In this sentence, probably as you say the 'T' of the word 'terribly' or perhaps on the 'P' of the word 'important', depending on what you want to stress.

Use facial expressions consciously

Nature has equipped you with a wonderful device for expressing all sorts of emotions – your face. You have been using this device all your life, so you don't need any advice from me on how to use it. Nor do you need me to tell you how to read other people's expressions. The only point I want to make here is that you should not overlook the importance of facial expressions – you can make gestures even when your hands are in your pockets, by changing your expression.

You can express all sorts of things with your face and movements of your head and shoulders: a shrug on its own means one thing, but a slightly slower shrug accompanied by a lifting of the eyebrows and a slight tilt of the head means something quite different.

The same rules apply here as for gestures: if you are talking in a large room, you need to be larger than life. Make sure that people can see your expressions. Similarly make sure that your timing is right. For example, saying the words 'You're a right crook' with a smile on your face is quite different from saying 'You're a right crook' and smiling a second or so later. It might be too late, you might already be on the seat of your pants!

Use body language appropriately

This is not the place to go into a detailed discussion of body language and what it means, though it is a fascinating subject and you may like to read more about it for yourself. Here again, our conditioning has taught us to read the language, even though we do it unconsciously. However, there are some subtle differences between cultures. For example, when a Greek person nods his head, does he mean 'yes' or 'no'?

On the whole, if you are talking to someone from your own culture, your interpretation of their body language (and their interpretation of yours) is likely to be reasonably accurate. Again, you will be using an established language, so use it consciously, but be larger than life. If you would normally lean forward when you are stressing a point, make sure that your lean can be seen.

If you are feeling nervous and you do not do anything to control your body language, you will be sending out unconscious signals that betray the fact – your head may be slightly bowed, your shoulders hunched a little, your knees slightly flexed and you may want to clasp and unclasp your hands. In these circumstances it does not matter how confident you *sound*. If your body language contradicts what you are saying then, at best, you may be sending confusing messages to your audience. At worst, your body language might completely undermine your good oral work.

So here too, bearing in mind that you are already fluent in the language, send messages that conform with your words.

Stand up straight, with shoulders back and head tilted slightly upward. You will then be sending a coherent message, which will increase the audience's confidence in you and your confidence in yourself.

If you want your audience to participate in what you are doing, by answering questions for example, you can encourage them to do so by attaching the right body language to the words. For example, imagine yourself sitting in the audience at a presentation. The speaker is standing very erect, in an almost military pose, and suddenly, he or she frowns and barks a question at you: 'What do you think of the show so far!?'

Now imagine that the speaker, with raised eyebrows and a smile, leans slightly toward you and with hunched shoulders and with arms bent and palms upward asks: 'What do you think of the show so far!?'

Which of these will encourage you to participate? From my own experience, the second approach generally works best.

This is a fairly typical example of how you can use body language positively to do a specific job. And there are many other occasions when the appropriate use of body language can help you get your message across more efficiently and effectively.

Use your position in the room consciously

This section applies particularly to those occasions when you are addressing more than ten to fifteen people. Incidentally, a group of five or six people reacts quite differently from a group of fifteen and a group of fifty people reacts differently again. Depending on the size of the room or hall, an audience of a hundred plus reacts in yet another way, though beyond a hundred or so it does not seem to change much.

In very general terms, a large audience seems to react as one (though that may be simply because there are too many people to monitor individually). A group of five or six, on the other hand, is a collection of individuals, there is no hiding place and it is sometimes quite difficult to generate a 'group spirit' which welds them into one. With a group of fifteen to twenty-five or so the group is small enough to allow interaction, but large enough for people to remain anonymous – if you let them – and also large enough for them to begin to react as one. So, in many ways, working with this size group can be more rewarding for all concerned, even though it is the most taxing to control.

In this section I want to concentrate on how you might handle a group of fifteen to twenty-five. Most of the underlying principles will remain the same for other size groups, but the techniques for implementing them will usually be different. Bear in mind that with this size of group it is probably best to arrange the seating in a U-shape, with the speaking position in the open end of the U.

You can control many things simply by the way you position yourself in the room. For instance, if you have been speaking from behind a table or a lectern and you want to find out if your points have been absorbed, you may decide to ask a question of the group. The fact that you are standing (i.e. you are higher up than the members of the audience) and you are behind a barrier (the table or lectern) puts you in a position of authority. But by asking a question you are, in a sense, handing over that authority to whoever answers the question. Somehow you will have to signal to the group that this is what you want to do. You can do this in various ways:

- Having posed the question from your position of authority, simply move to one side, so the barrier is no longer between you and the audience.

- If an answer is slow in coming, try moving towards the group, thus crossing the invisible fence created by the barrier. With this movement you are saying, 'Right, I'm one of you now, so speak up.'

- If you want to open things up for a wider discussion, try moving in front of the barrier and sitting down – either on the group side of the desk, or, for really informal sessions, on a chair you have placed on the audience's side of the barrier.

- The movements also work in reverse. When you think it is time to end a discussion – even an informal discussion – simply stand to signal that you are taking back some of the authority. Move behind the barrier again to signal that it is time to move on.

All these movements must appear perfectly natural and unhurried. If you scuttle from one position to another like a frightened spider you will not create the desired effect; it will seem planned and contrived – which, of course, it should be – but you don't want the audience to know that.

Let us consider another example. This time, assume that you have been standing on the audience side of the barrier making a fairly informal, relaxed presentation and two people at the back start to hold a private conversation. What should you do? You are not in the correct position and the group is not in the right mood for you to impose authority, so shouting at them won't work.

Instead, say nothing, but look pointedly at the two people holding the conversation. The silence will build up a pressure in the room which will be noticed first of all by the people who are paying attention. They in turn will look at the conversationalists, also remaining silent. It will not be long before one of the two people will feel the pressure of the silence and look up. This is usually the point at which the conversation ends. You can assist the process by saying something like, 'Did you want to make a point Fred?' (Assuming it's a man and his name is in fact Fred.)

If one of them insists on continuing with the chat, then move slowly towards him or her. In our culture, there is a point about two feet away from someone where their personal space, or 'territory', ends. If you stand just outside that boundary you will usually catch their attention, and they will look up sheepishly. Your superior height will do the rest. This is a position of confrontation, so as soon as the person looks up, smile, say something like 'I was just being nosy', and back off, making your next point as you go.

If the person still insists on continuing, then you will have to go through with the confrontation. You will have to cross the boundary of their territory, to within about a foot, so you loom over them. Interrupt politely with, 'Excuse me Fred, we need to carry on.' And once you have made your point back off again.

When you are standing at the front of the audience try to imagine invisible lines of interaction between yourself and each member of the group. It is your job to keep those lines open for everyone in the room.

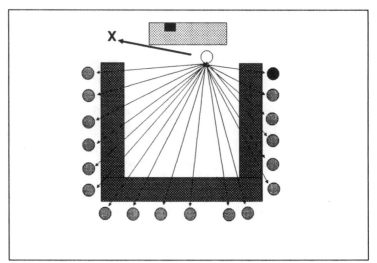

8-1   Plan view of a U-shaped seating arrangement, showing imaginary lines of interaction between the presenter and the audience.

For instance, if you are standing to one side of the U-shape (as in the diagram above) and someone near you, at the front, asks you a question, there is a danger that, in your rush to be helpful, you will break some of the lines, or at least stretch them unbearably. If you turn to the questioner, you might well have your back to people on the other side of the U. Also, if you are standing quite near to the person asking the question, it is likely that they will speak in a low voice, which means that other people in the room may not hear it. All in all, this situation can create problems.

The textbooks say that when someone asks you a question from the floor, you should repeat the question in your own words to ensure that you have understood it correctly and to ensure that other members of the group hear it before you start answering. This is very sound advice, and I wish I could do it, but I always forget. Instead I have developed another device which might work for you too.

As the person (marked in black in Figure 8-1) begins to ask the question I slowly move away from them (towards point X in the diagram) with a thoughtful expression on my face. This has to be done gently and naturally. It can be a bit disconcerting for a questioner if you zap across to the other side of the room as soon as you are spoken to! But executed properly, this movement does two things: firstly it opens up the lines of communication to all the other members of the group and secondly, as you move away the questioner will automatically raise his or her voice, which means that the other members of the group will hear the question for themselves.

As with all the other unspoken communicators we have discussed in this chapter, using your position in the room to do specific things is something which will come fairly naturally. And don't forget that the same principles apply to all sorts of situations. So, for example, the next time you are trying to persuade someone to do something, don't do it across a desk. Find an excuse for sitting next to them (perhaps to look at some figures). Your position relative to theirs will carry lots of signals – you will literally be on their side.

Now you know what to look out for when you are assessing a speaker's performance, practise as much as you can. We can all learn a lot from other speakers – but only if we see them in action. Watch some of the many awards programmes on the television to see how the prize-winners perform as themselves, watch clips of speeches on the news, watch debates in the House of Commons and try to judge whether the speakers are good or bad at communicating verbally.

Then comes the difficult bit – try to assess *why* they are good or bad. The checklists in this book will help you.

9 You and the audience

Much of your success as a speaker will depend on your relationship with the audience and their relationship with you. If you remember, right at the start of this book I said: if you want to be successful, make the needs of your audience your major criterion. *Always!* By now you should have an idea of just how fundamental that point is.

You may also have noticed that, for the speaker, giving a talk is actually a long line of decisions. He or she has to decide on the purpose, the objectives, the information needed by the audience, the best way to structure the information, the best medium to use and so on... Success here depends on you being able to make the right decisions as you prepare the talk.

But what you do while you are actually *giving* the talk is also important. If you can see things through the eyes of your audience, you will be able to think on your feet and make the right decisions as you go along. This chapter covers some of the more general things you will have to take into account while you are speaking, though, as usual, it all starts well before you give the talk. You have to adopt the right 'mind set' (to use a buzz phrase). Once in that mind set you will make decisions naturally.

You and the audience

Checklist

Aims and expectations

☐ Know your attitude towards the audience

☐ Know the audience's requirements of you

☐ Try to inform, persuade and entertain, not impress

Tailor your presentation

☐ Use appropriate language

☐ Use examples from your own experience and analogies from theirs

☐ Involve the whole audience

AIMS AND EXPECTATIONS

■■■■■■ Know your attitude towards the audience

This probably sounds like a silly thing to have as the first heading in a checklist. After all we know our attitude towards the audience: they scare us witless!

I jest, of course, but there is a serious point here. Just before I start any presentation I try to put myself in the audience's shoes. How would I feel in their place? What would I expect from the session? Will I have had time to read the briefing notes before I came? What will motivate me to do as the speaker asks?

Understanding your audience's feelings is one thing, *feeling* as a member of the audience feels is quite different. It is the difference between sympathy and empathy. The successful speaker will empathise with his or her audience. Once you have thought yourself into your audience's shoes you are less likely to make silly mistakes, to make unwarranted assumptions, or behave in a thoughtless way. In short you will automatically tailor what you say and do to meet their needs.

If you, in their position, would need encouragement to participate, then you are more likely to provide that encouragement. If you would not be able to see the point of the talk, you are more likely to express the purpose in terms which they will be able to accept. If you would be antagonistic towards the whole thing, then you are more likely to take steps to overcome or divert that antagonism.

We must never assume that just because we have been asked to give a talk, the audience will actually want to listen. We have to make them want to listen. And we can do that best if we understand what makes them tick. So try to think as they would.

■■■■■■ Know the audience's requirements of you

The first question to ask yourself is, 'If I were a member of this audience, what would I expect of the speaker?' Their inner thoughts will vary from audience to audience and from talk to talk, but here are a couple of examples of the 'typical' answers you might formulate if you, like me, had to present a course called 'Successful Presentations':

■ *For senior executives of a bank*
In their place I would expect the speaker to:

- Be highly professional.
- Have wide experience of public speaking.
- Be confident and relaxed.
- Understand my working environment (but not my job).
- Dress and behave as I do.
- Understand business, but not necessarily finance.
- Understand the particular difficulties created by my job.
- Show me how to stop being nervous.
- Provide hand-outs which contain practical guidelines and rules for speaking in public.
- Be able to tell me what I'm doing wrong, without making me look foolish.
- Show me how to deal with hostile audiences.

■ *The same topic for proprietors of small businesses*

- Be professional, but helpful.
- Have wide experience of public speaking.
- Be confident and capable.
- Know about the practicalities of running a business.
- Know how to deal with the full range of situations I might encounter.
- Be able to provide practical help.
- Show me the tricks of the trade.
- Tell me what to do.

If you look carefully at the two lists, you will see that they both contain broadly the same items, even though they are expressed in different terms. This is because the audiences approach the course from slightly different standpoints.

The bank executives know that making verbal presentations is an unavoidable part of their jobs. They will have had previous experience of making presentations and they will either have nagging doubts about their abilities, or they will be looking for ways to make it less of a chore. Some of the course members will already be very accomplished speakers, but have no way of judging their performance. And there will be some who *are* confident of their abilities, but are looking for ways to improve further. Quite a mixed audience.

The small business proprietors, on the other hand, may be attending the course simply because they have a vague feeling that it might help them sell, do the 'right things' in meetings, or negotiate better contracts. Many of them will have no previous experience at all. Some may have had to give a talk at Round Table, or to their local Chamber of Commerce – and hated every second of it. Again, quite a mixed audience – but different from the bankers.

Once you know how the audience is likely to view the topic, and what they want to get from the presentation, you are in a better position to tailor it to their needs. You are less likely to talk 'over the heads' of the less knowledgeable, or to patronise those who do have previous experience.

If you were to present a different topic to these same audiences (say, 'Interest Rates'), the audience expectations would be different again. It is vital that you remember that. And it is only prudent to work out what you would be expecting if you were in their shoes. The important thing is that you analyse these things before you begin to design your presentation, but don't waste your efforts by letting it end there. You will find it very useful to review your list again – just before you start your talk; it will help you prepare yourself mentally for the job in hand.

Try to inform, persuade and entertain, not impress

Speakers who set out to satisfy themselves rather than their audiences rarely communicate well. You have only got to look at television advertisements to see some examples for yourself. There are some which are stunningly beautiful, use the very latest lighting techniques and the most fashionable designers, and have casts of thousands in a dazzling display of special effects, yet somehow it is difficult to see what they are driving at. What is worse, you sometimes can't remember the name of the product or company they are selling.

There is a similar phenomenon with people who speak in public. In extreme cases, they arrive on site with ranks of slide projectors, smoke machines, video inserts and typeset hand-outs. Their delivery is flawless – obviously rehearsed to perfection – and yet...

My reaction when I see presentations such as this is to feel slightly affronted. 'I have come to listen to this person and he or she cannot have tailored the presentation for my needs. This is a roadshow, a circus, propaganda! They are not talking to me, they are talking to some notional idea of what they think I should be!' And I cannot help feeling that the presenter could have more respect for me and for the other people in the audience.

In my view the speaker's job is very much like that of an actor: it is their job to research the material and then to become a vehicle for the words and ideas. A good actor merges into the part and into the action. If you come away from a theatre remembering a particular actor, then perhaps you should be suspicious of that actor's performance and of his or her reasons for playing the part. You have to look very hard to see a great actor acting. A great actor has the courage (and the confidence) to submerge his or her own ego and let the 'message' take centre stage.

This might be why amateur dramatics are sometimes so bad. If you have two or three members of a cast who are determined to get what *they* can from the performance, then it must detract from the contributions of the other actors and from the power of the play. You will have seen the sort of people I mean; they are the grinning buffoons who always seem to be where the spotlight is and, on the few occasions when they are not blinking in the glare, they are posing artistically in the background.

Put bluntly, if your audience comes away from your talk remembering you, rather than what you said, then you have failed in your job.

You don't need to worry over-much about how you will look on the day, whether you will make mistakes, whether you will gain the respect of the audience. Instead you should worry about getting the message across, achieving the objectives, fulfilling the audience's needs and helping them to gain information or make up their minds. If you concentrate too hard on polishing the radio, there won't be enough time to transmit the whole message.

TAILOR YOUR PRESENTATION

Use appropriate language

Once again, the key word here is 'appropriate' – appropriate, that is, to the audience and the subject matter. The implication is that you will have to be prepared to modify the language you used for one audience when you speak to another. That does take a bit of discipline and you may need the help of a friend or colleague to do it. It is very easy, for example, to get all enthusiastic about your topic and start thinking and talking in your own specialist language. We have all heard computer buffs rabbiting on about 'RAMs' and 'megabytes' and 'floppies' and 'software', but specialist terms such as these do little to aid communication with novices. It is very easy to slip into specialist language, particularly as you settle down and relax. Yet the decision-making process involved in choosing appropriate language is very much a matter of common sense, provided you take the time to think about it. In most cases you will know whether or not to use trade jargon, whether your audience will understand certain phrases, and so on.

Of course, using the right language involves much more than simply choosing the right words. You need to be sure that your 'preferred style' of speaking has certain characteristic features. If your preferred style is basically sound then it will be easier to modify it for a particular audience. So what characterises a good general-purpose style? Here are some suggestions:

■ Keep your sentences short and simple

'Long convoluted excursions like this sentence, which contain sub-clauses, even sub-sub-clauses, in which you start talking and then amble around, seemingly without a real purpose, leave the audience, who will be waiting patiently, confused.' This could be expressed much more efficiently and effectively as, 'Convoluted sentences confuse the audience.'

■ *Use the active voice, rather than the passive voice*

Instead of saying, 'Short sentences should be used', say, 'Use short sentences.' The second of the sentences (the one in the active voice) is punchier and it leaves us in no doubt as to who should perform the action: '[You should] use short sentences.' Whereas in the first example it is not immediately clear who should use short sentences.

■ *Use familiar words*

This one is often – in fact usually – mistranslated to mean use short words. 'Marmalade' is more than twice as big as 'iamb'[1], but which is the more familiar? Use words which your audience will find familiar and do not worry too much if it is a long word or a short word. All things being equal, use Anglo-Saxon words, because they are more immediate than those of Greek, Latin or French origin, as well as being a little less pretentious sounding.

■ *Use familiar ideas*

In some ways this is more important than using familiar words. If a word is unfamiliar to us, we can always look in a dictionary. But where do we go for help if we don't understand an idea? People often make the mistake (and I think an arrogant one) of setting out to give a talk which is an 'idiots guide' to their topic. This is a mistake for a couple of reasons: firstly, the audience are seldom idiots and should never be treated as such even if they are. Secondly, people sometimes use childish language instead of adult language in the belief that the words will unravel the mystery. If the point you are making is founded on assumptions or facts which are unknown to the audience, then it does not matter how simple you make the language, they won't be able to see the point. It is like trying to make a chain out of small links rather than big ones. If any of the links (big or small) is missing, you will never be able to construct a whole chain.

■ *Use concrete rather than abstract ideas*

For example, in the previous paragraph I used the analogy of a chain, because it illustrates the idea of links being bound together. I also used it because it is a concrete image which can be instantly recognised by the vast majority of people reading this book. The analogy created a

1 My dictionary defines 'iamb' as, 'Prosody: a metrical foot of two syllables'. Does that make us any the wiser?

recognisable image to illustrate a very abstract idea. And all this leads on rather nicely to the next point.

Use examples from your own experience and analogies from theirs

Examples and analogies are useful because they illustrate or reinforce the point you are trying to make. They can also provide added insight quickly and painlessly. And one of the things we are trying to do is to make our talk entertaining, so we might include anecdotes in our tool kit as well. Make sure that you have a good stock of all three, because they bring the topic to life for the audience. Examples and anecdotes are also a crafty way of demonstrating your own experience, though do not overdo it because you might start sounding like 'The Great I Am': 'Back in 1980 when I was running one of these sessions in Athens...' This might impress some people, but it can also prompt the response: 'Well if you're that good, what are you doing here talking to the likes of me!?'

Wherever possible make sure that the examples and anecdotes are real and from your own experience. Made-up examples quite often lead to trouble, simply because you cannot know all the factors involved. You are constantly saying, 'Well if, then...' which is not very satisfactory, nor is it convincing. It is suspect because it is contrived and it is always open to the retort, 'If? *If!* If your auntie had a deep voice she'd be your uncle!'

Imaginary examples or ones you have heard about or read in a book are not good enough for most purposes. An innocent question about a point of detail can entirely destroy your carefully constructed competent, experienced and capable image. It can leave you red-faced with your trousers round your ankles when you have to admit that you don't really know what caused the sequence of events, or how the vicar came to be involved in the first place. For some topics you will be forced to use made-up examples, but use them carefully.

Where analogies are concerned you must be sure that the analogy is one which the people in your audience are likely to have encountered. If you are explaining, for example, to an audience of chefs, how gears work, you could use all sorts of analogies, but the best one is probably that of a rotary whisk. If, on the other hand, you were explaining the same thing to some schoolchildren, then perhaps a bicycle might be a good analogy, where the up and down movement of the legs is converted into the rotary motion of the wheels.

▉▉▉▉▉▉▉ Involve the whole audience

There is a lot of stage terminology in this book. And this is no accident. Speaking formally, particularly to larger groups, involves quite a lot of showmanship and stagecraft. We can learn a lot simply by watching actors do their job: using the voice, using gestures, using facial expressions, even using silence. We can see all these on our televisions every night, though we must remember that television is a very small-scale, intimate medium. The techniques used on television are designed to work with an audience of three or four people who know each other and are sitting in their own living room.

Acting on a stage or talking to a larger group is different. The action takes place on neutral ground and the 'dynamics' of the audience are different. So therefore the techniques have to be different too. As we have seen, gestures must be larger if they are to be seen by all the audience. But other less obvious things have to change as well.

A large audience offers plenty of hiding places for people who don't want to be involved, and it is easy to 'lose' one or more members of the audience. You therefore need to take positive action to monitor what is happening in the group and then be ready to take remedial action if someone seems to be slipping away from you. Ideally, you should try to ensure that nobody *can* slip away whether you notice or not.

Attention span is the crucial factor here. I don't know how long you can keep your concentration on a speaker – it probably depends on how good the speaker is – but I have seen estimates of the average attention span which range from as low as two minutes to as high as twenty minutes. Being a pessimist, and just in case they are right, I have always taken the worst case figure of two minutes as my guideline. I reason that if you are talking to a group of, say, ten people, then right at the beginning of the session all ten will be at the peak of attention. They will be bright-eyed and ready to go. As the talk progresses their attention will gradually wane, or perhaps something the speaker says will trigger off another thought. This will happen to all ten people, but at different rates. So, after a couple of minutes we have a situation where some of the audience will be listening and absorbing information, some will be thinking about the shopping while they are listening and others will be sitting on a beach in the south of France.

After a few moments the beach people will realise what is happening and begin to drift back into the presentation. Meanwhile the shoppers have reached their beach and the ones who were paying attention are beginning to construct shopping lists. And so people drift in and out of the talk at different rates according to their particular attention cycle. It follows that when the speaker presents a key point for the one and only time, a good proportion of the audience will miss the point entirely. You cannot let this happen to you. So, how do you avoid it? You will have to do a number of things and I have listed some of them below.

- ### *Make key points more than once*
  The old training handbooks used to say that you should make a key point three times, using different words each time, but there is no magic formula. I believe the training maxim I quoted earlier is a better method: 'First, tell 'em what you're going to tell 'em. Then tell 'em. Then tell 'em what you've told 'em.' Or in our terms, introduce the key point, present the key point, then summarise and re-state the key point. If you do nothing else, spreading it out like this will at least give you a better chance of catching everyone at the top of their cycle at some time.

- ### *How to involve the audience*
  Ideally, you will involve them by getting them to do some task or other. If the topic does not allow this, then at least ask them questions. If either the topic or the size of the audience precludes this, then pepper your talk with rhetorical questions. They add interest and take people by surprise: 'Is he asking me that question!?'

■ *Change the scenery*

In short, do anything reasonable and natural seeming to break into the audience's cycle of attention and inattention: move about on the stage, walk from side to side, walk towards and away from the group, display a visual aid, sit down, stand up again, tell a joke, give an example, recount an anecdote, drop a pen on the desk. There are lots of devices and you will need them all, because you will have to provide a change of scenery at frequent and irregular intervals throughout your talk.

■ *Give summaries*

Summaries are a very useful tool. Use them at the end of each major stage of the talk as well as at the end of particular key points.

■ *Maintain 'eye contact'*

This will convince people that you are speaking to them personally and they will usually be too polite to let themselves drift off.

■ *Vary your 'intensity level'*

At some times be keen and emphatic, at others matter-of-fact and conciliatory. Variety is of the essence. After a fairly short while, someone ranting away like Hitler is just as boring and soporific as a tired actuary reading the phone book out loud.

■ *Monitor what is happening in the audience*

This is the best reason for maintaining eye contact. But beware, some people who spend a lot of time in meetings and listening to talks have perfected the art of appearing to be wide awake and concentrating hard on what you say while inside they are unpacking the shopping in the beach house and drinking an ice-cold beer.

They are very difficult to spot, but there are some telltale signs. For instance, when someone is genuinely concentrating they tend to move their eyes and eyebrows – perhaps frowning slightly for a brief moment. If they don't quite see a point they tend to rotate their eyes upwards and to one side until they make the connection, then the eyes will move back to the centre again. If you see a member of the audience sitting muppet-like with a fixed stare and a motionless forehead you have reason to suspect that no one's in. Keep an eye on the person and if there is no change after a couple of minutes, use one of the scenery-changing techniques I mentioned earlier.

- ### *End on a high point*

Audiences need a clear beginning and a clear end to the presentation. It must seem whole, complete and properly rounded. But, if you can achieve your objectives and at the same time awaken the audience's desire to find out more, then that is real success. The show-biz expression is, 'Leave them wanting more', and that is a laudable aim. But you should never leave them *needing* more. Have the confidence that your audience will want to know more and finish off your presentation by summarising the whole talk in a sentence or two, by drawing conclusions for the audience and then telling them where they can find out more.

In fact I propose that you have a *closing* ritual as well as an opening ritual. Remember, 'P B S' at the beginning and 'S C M' (Summary, Conclusions, More) at the end.

- ### *Assessing your own performance*

A successful presentation is one where the people in the audience feel that they have had 'good value for money' and the presenter knows that the objectives have been achieved. Don't try to assess your own performance immediately after the session. If you have put your heart into the job you will probably feel drained and slightly depressed as the audience files out. I know I do. We have all been in the position of remembering our best joke on the way home from the party, and a similar thing happens after your talk: you will remember the small points you wanted to make, but forgot; the examples you wanted to quote; the analogies you meant to draw, and many other little things which might *(might)* have added an extra polish to your performance. Leave at least a day before trying to measure how well you have done, so you can see things in their true perspective.

By all means ask the audience for their comments immediately after the presentation has ended, but ask them to give them in writing on a standard form. This will ensure that the audience all answer the same questions and approach the criticism in a controlled, if not objective, way. Their responses will usually be expressed as opinions and you must not fall into the trap of reading too much into them. It is perfectly possible for the audience to like you, to be impressed by the job you have done and yet be unable to do what your objectives stated they should be able to do.

Of course, if the purpose of your talk has been to alter the audience's opinions, then the best way to check this out is to ask them for their opinions about the topic. But if the purpose was to *inform* them about something, they may feel quite sincerely that they have been informed, but this is not an objective measure of how much they know about the topic.

This chapter has been about the way that you interact with the audience during your presentation. It reinforces the point that the audience is all important. From the time you first discover that you have to make a presentation, right through to the moment when you walk from the room with the applause ringing in your ears, it is they who should determine your every decision about the session. And it is their responses in the ensuing days which will tell you if you did a good job or not.

The customers are always right – even if they don't know it.

10 Putting it all together

It is all very well reading things in a book, but when the crunch comes how do you go about creating and presenting your talk? What is the first thing you should do? And then what...?

In this chapter I have put together all the checklists. They summarise what I would see as the normal sequence of events. This is what I would do and this is what I have advised many many other people to do.

The procedures work for me. They worked for them and I am pretty sure that they can work for you too. Give them a try.

Good luck with your talks.

Checklist

Step 1: Examine your fears

☐ What precisely is the fear?

☐ How likely is it to happen and what will you do if it does?

Step 2: Prepare yourself

☐ Know your role and your reasons for talking

Step 3: Starting to speak

☐ Regulate your breathing

☐ Relax your face and neck muscles

☐ Establish eye contact

☐ Occupy your hands

☐ Start your opening ritual

Preparing your talk

Checklist

Research

☐ Define the purpose

☐ Know your audience

☐ Define objectives

☐ Know the setting and conditions

Analyse

☐ Analyse the subject matter in the light of all the above

Structuring your talk

Checklist

The framework

☐ Identify the main elements and sub-elements of the topic

☐ Choose a starting point

☐ Find the 'best' route through the material

Movable parts

☐ Find analogies to clarify unfamiliar ideas

☐ Use examples and illustrations to support the message

Memory aids

Checklist

☐ Prepare a 'route map' through the topic

☐ Identify key words and phrases

☐ Prepare your notes

☐ Prepare support materials

Support materials

Checklist

Preparing the material

☐ Have a clear purpose for the material

☐ Make sure that the material is clear and legible

☐ Use layout as part of the message

Using the material

☐ Know when to use the material

☐ Make sure that everyone can see the material

Starting your talk

Checklist

Before the presentation

☐ Check location of power points and extension leads

☐ Check that all equipment works and that there are no trailing leads or other hazards

☐ Get spare bulbs, pens, pads, chalk, etc

☐ Arrange seating

☐ Check that presentation notes are to hand

☐ Check that samples, diagrams and hand-outs are available

☐ Check location of fire exits and toilets

☐ Check lunch/coffee/tea arrangements

☐ Make final preparations

First impressions

☐ Take control from the outset

☐ Establish contact with the group (immediately)

☐ Go through your opening ritual

Using your voice

Checklist

Voice control

☐ Control your breathing

☐ Project, don't shout

☐ Vary the pitch, tone and volume

☐ Don't swallow the ends of words and sentences

Speaking techniques

☐ Use pauses for punctuation

☐ Use questions

Looking good

Checklist

☐ Take control and keep it

☐ Manage your mannerisms

☐ Use gestures appropriately

☐ Use facial expressions consciously

☐ Use body language appropriately

☐ Use your position in the room consciously

You and the audience

Checklist

Aims and expectations

☐ Know your attitude towards the audience

☐ Know the audience's requirements of you

☐ Try to inform, persuade and entertain, not impress

Tailor your presentation

☐ Use appropriate language

☐ Use examples from your own experience and analogies from theirs

☐ Involve the whole audience

YOUR OWN NOTES